The Seven Feasts of Israel

Historical and Prophetic Significance

Don T. Phillips

"The Seven Feasts of Israel: Historical and Prophetic Significance," by Don T. Phillips. ISBN 978-1-63868-151-9.

Published 2023 by Virtualbookworm.com Publishing Inc., P.O. Box 9949, College Station, TX 77845, US. Copyright ©2023 Don T. Phillips.

All rights reserved. No part of this publication may be reproduced, stored in a retrieval system, or transmitted in any form or by any means, electronic, mechanical, recording or otherwise, without the prior written permission of Don T. Phillips.

Table of Contents

Part I: The 7 Feasts of Israel: Introduction 1

   The Hebrew calendar 2

Part II: The Spring Feasts of Israel 6

   Feast of Passover 6

      Messianic Application 9

   Feast of Unleavened Bread 17

      Messianic Application 21

   Feast of Firstfruits 24

      Messianic Application 32

         The Women Visit the Tomb 43

   Feast of Shavuot 51

      Messianic Application 56

   Summary of the First Four (Spring) Feasts of Israel 64

Part III: The Fall Feasts of Israel 69

   Feast of Rosh Hashanah 73

      Messianic Application 77

         The Royal Coronation 84

         Rapture of the Saints 84

            The Last Trump 88

         The Bride of Christ 89

   Feast of Yom Kippur 95

      Messianic Application 96

  The 1000-Year millennial Kingdom 99

  The Jewish Messiah 100

  All of Israel Will be Saved 101

  The Day of the Lord 103

 Feast of Tabernacles 105

  Lighting Candles 107

  The 8th Day 108

  The Water Pouring Ceremony 108

  The Lights 110

 Messianic Application 110

  The Pool of Silom 110

  The Coronation of Jesus Christ 111

  Future Feast of Tabernacles 112

Part IV: The Future Revealed **114**

 The Rapture 114

 The Battle of Armageddon 115

 The Last Feast 116

BIBLIOGRAPHY **119**

Part I

The Seven Feasts of Israel: *Introduction*

It is impossible to correctly understand the sequence of end-time events without understanding the historical and prophetic meaning of the *Seven Feasts of Israel*. They provide a blueprint for both the 1st and the 2nd comings of Jesus Christ. The Seven Feasts of Israel were ordained by God shortly after the law was given at Mt. Sinai following the Exodus from Egypt. They were given for two reasons. The *first* was to commemorate the deliverance of Israel from Egyptian bondage and slavery. The *second* was to prophesy of Seven events which will herald the first and second coming of Jesus Christ. The first four Feasts are held in the Spring, and the last three in the Fall. The first four Feasts were fulfilled at the death and resurrection of Jesus Christ. The last three will be fulfilled as the 70th week of Daniel and the current Church Age comes to a close.

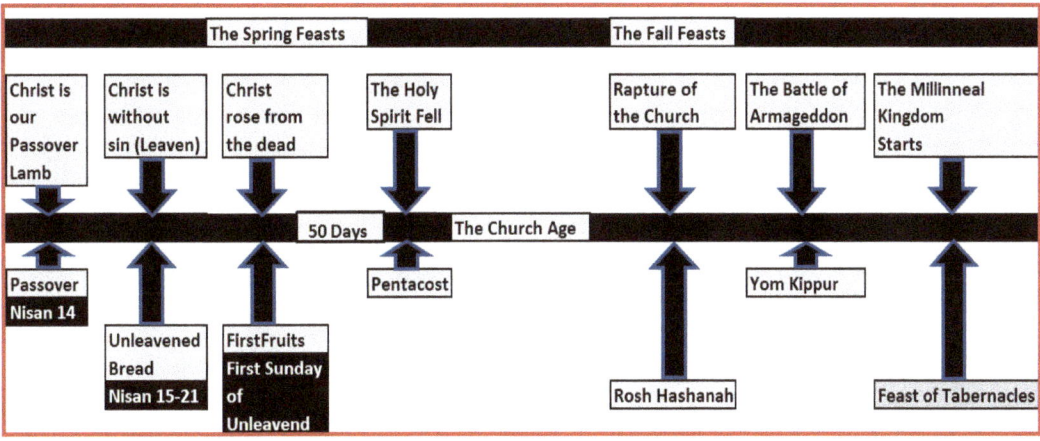

The Seven Feasts and their appointed time on the Hebrew calendar are shown in the following table.

	Feast	Hebrew Dates
1	Passover (Pesah)	Nisan 14
2	Unleavened Bread	Nisan 15-Nisan 21
3	Firstfruits	Only Sunday during Feast of Unleavened Bread
4	Pentecost (Weeks)	50 Day count starting on the only Sunday which falls in The Feast of Unleavened Bread
5	Trumpets (Rosh Hashanna)	Tishri 1
6	Yom Kippu (Atoneent)	Tishri 10
7	Tabernacles (Booths)	Tishri 15-Tishri 22

The Hebrew Calendar

The *Basic* Hebrew calendar is a *lunar* calendar. It is composed of 12 months alternating between 29 and 30 days per month. Each month starts on the new moon. From new moon to new moon is approximately 29.5306 days. Since days must be whole numbers, it is obvious why they alternated between 29 and 30 days in length. Note that a *basic* 12-month year was 354 days long.

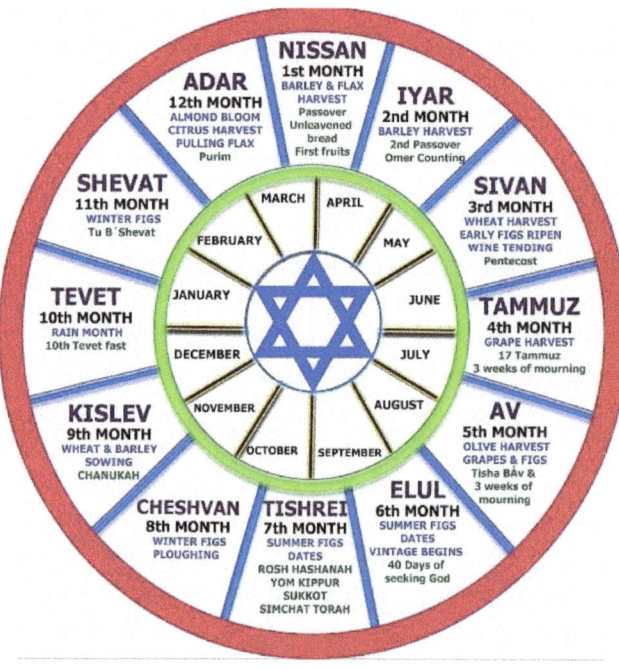

This causes a problem because a year is determined not by the moon, but by the sun, and a *solar year* is about 365 days in length (365.2422 days). Without some sort of adjustment, the Hebrew 354-day, 12-month year would *fall behind* a solar year at a rate of about 11.25 days every year. In other words, if unadjusted about every 17 years a Fall festival would occur in the Spring! It was determined long ago that to keep the two calendars (lunar and solar) in sync with one another, a 13th month of 29/30 days, called Adar II, was inserted Seven times over a 19-year cycle. Adar II was always inserted after the month of Adar. In addition, the 1st 6 (Spring) months were fixed to alternate between 30 and 29 days, and an extra day is periodically added to selected Fall months to keep the 1st day of every month in sync with a new moon. These periodic adjustments enabled the Lunar Hebrew year of 360 days to remain fairly close to a Solar Gregorian year of 365.2425 Gregorian days. The modified, original Hebrew Calendar proved to be very accurate, but because an extra month was periodically inserted after the month of Adar (called Adar II), and extra days are added as needed to the basic 360-day Hebrew Calendar year, the date of each of the Seven Feasts wandered between two months of the Gregorian Calendar months. For example, Tishri 1 would some years fall in September and some in October. The ancient Hebrew calendar has always used sophisticated rules to regulate the yearly calendar and keep it in sync with a solar year, but each feast date still *wanders* across two months. Even so, the ancient Herew calendar which is still in use today is remarkably accurate over a 19-year cycle. The additional month of Adar II is added every 3rd, 6th, 8th, 11th, 14th, 17th, and 19th years in a designated 19-year cycle. These additional months are called *Leap Months* and a year with an extra month is called a *Leap Year*. Properly adjusted during the 7 Fall months, every 19-years each date of a New Moon coincides almost exactly on both the Lunar and solar calendars. This 19-year repeating cycle is called a *Metonic Cycle*.

Modern computer programmers and NASA scientist have written computer programs to accurately calculate the month, date and day of the week on both the Hebrew and the Gregorian calendars back through thousands of years. We will not elaborate further on the operation of the Jewish calendar, but it is a fascinating and rewarding study. We will now concentrate on what each festival means, both historically and prophetically, and refer to when each festival occurs by its Jewish name and Jewish calendar date. There is, however, one important historical event which we must explain. God renumbered the Hebrew calendar months at the exodus from Egypt. Before the Exodus from Egypt, the month of Tishri was designated as the 1st month in a Jewish year. After the Exodus, Nisan 1 was designated by God to be the 1st month of the year. This caused no real calendar problems; it only renumbered the Jewish Calendar months. The Hebrew calendar has existed since ancient time. The Book of *Jubilees* records that Enoch *understood* the movement of the sun, moon and stars and was told by angels how calendars operate. In the flood account recorded in Genesis, it is clear that a calendar was in use. Moving forward in time, when the Children of Israel were in Egypt before the Exodus, there was a different Egyptian calendar. It consisted of 12 months of 30 days, and at the end of every year five extra days were added. This made an Egyptian year 365 days long, so it only dropped back from the solar year about one day every four years. Even this eventually made a large difference, and an extra day was addend every 4 years.

Before the Exodus, we have no definitive biblical records of what calendar was used by the Hebrews. However, after the Land of Canaan was conquered and divided among the 12 tribes, Israel became an agricultural nation and planted grain crops every year. The Spring *Feast of Firstfruits* had to occur just as the barley crop was maturing in the field, because the high priest had to *wave a Firstfruit* offering of barley before the Lord, and the Lord would have to bless the wave offering on the Feast of Firstfruits before anything could be harvested. It is clear that the month of Nisan was somehow started every year based upon how the crop was growing, possibly by observing the crop of barley as it matured and then inserting a 13th month in the previous year if the crop was not going to be ready for the Feast of Firstfruits which was observed on the only Sunday morning which fell in the *Feast of Unleavened Bread* (Nisan 15-Nisan 21).

Winding forward about 1000 years the southern kingdom of Judah fell to the Babylonian Empire. Virtually the whole nation was deported to Babylon for a period of 70 years for failing to observe Sabbatical and Jubilee years. The Babylonians had a deep knowledge of how calendars operated, and the Hebrews adopted the Babylonian names of each month with minor variations. We have biblical and historical records that confirm a sophisticated calendar was in effect and was being maintained by the Levitical priesthood soon after the Babylonian exile of 70 years had been completed.

As previously stated, the *Seven Feasts of Israel* are divided into two separate seasons of the year. The Feasts of *Passover*, *Firstfruits*, *Unleavened Bread* and *Pentecost* all take place in the Spring. The last three Feasts of *Rosh Hashanah*, *Yom Kippur*, and *Tabernacles* take place in the Fall. The Feasts have a dual meaning; they commemorate the deliverance of the Hebrew nation from Egyptian bondage, but they also prophesy of the first and second coming of Jesus Christ. The Hebrew word for feast is *moed* which means a *set time* or an *appointed time*. God has not only set an appointed time for each feast, he has also commanded that every male in Israel must be at the place of his choice (Jerusalem) for the Feasts of *Passover*, *Pentecost* and *Tabernacles*. The Feasts are also each called a *holy convocation*. The Hebrew word for convocation means *rehearsal*. The implication is that God has commanded the Children of Israel to observe each feast at the *appointed time* as *a rehearsal* for seven things which will happen to Israel on those days. Looking back, it is now obvious that Jesus Christ fulfilled the first four Feasts at His crucifixion between when He died on the cross of Calvary and when He sent the Holy Spirit to dwell in man on the Feast of Passover. The last three Feasts will be fulfilled at the second advent of Christ.

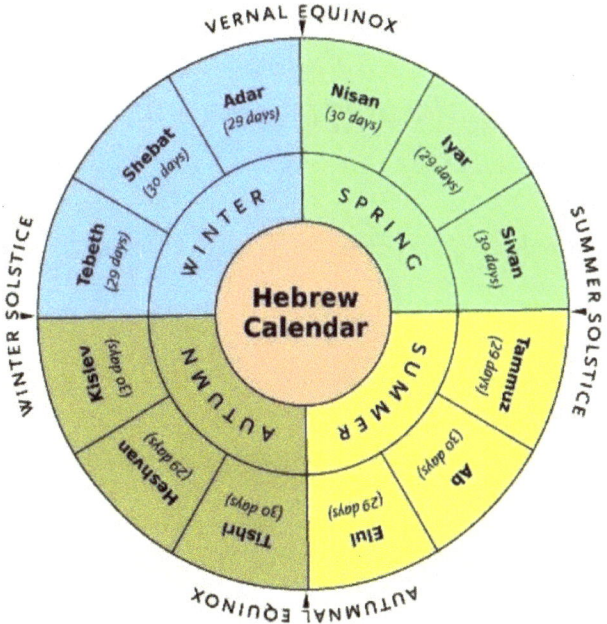

The Spring Feasts
(fulfilled @ Jesus' first coming)

Passover	Unleavened Bread	FirstFruits	Pentecost
Crucifixion Of Jesus	Burial Of Jesus	Resurrection Of Jesus	Coming of the Holy Spirit
Nisan 14	Nisan 15-22	Nisan 17	Sivan 7
Exodus 12 Matt 26:17-27	Lev 23:6-8 I Cor 5:7-8	Lev 23:9-14 I Cor 15:20-23	Lev 23:15-22 Acts 1 & 2

Part II
The Spring Feasts of Israel

Feast of Passover

The Feast of Passover is in remembrance of the day that the Hebrew nation left Egypt on Nisan 15 (Exodus 12:2-11). The Jewish day of Nisan 14 is often cited as the Feast of Passover, but this is a mistake made in the Western World and not by devout Jews. There is no feast on Nisan 14 nor is it a Holy Day. Nisan 14 is best defined as a preparation day for the High Holy day of Nisan 15, which is the 1st day of the *Feast of Unleavened Bread*.

*In the fourteenth day of the first month **at evening** is the LORD's Passover*   Leviticus 23:5

*[3] In the fourteenth day of this month, at even, **ye shall keep it in his appointed season**: according to all the rites of it, and according to all the ceremonies thereof, shall ye keep it.*
[4] And Moses spoke unto the children of Israel, that they should keep the Passover   Numbers 9: 3-4

On Nisan 10, God instructed the Children of Israel to select an unblemished lamb one year old and bring it into each house for four days.

[1] And the LORD spoke unto Moses and Aaron in the land of Egypt, saying,
*[2] **This month** (Nisan) **shall be unto you the beginning of months**: it shall be the first month of the year to you.*
*[3] Speak ye unto all the congregation of Israel, saying, **In the tenth day***

of this month *they shall take to them every man a lamb, according to the house of their fathers, a lamb for every house*
[6] *And **ye shall keep it up until the fourteenth day of the same month**: and the whole assembly of the congregation of Israel shall kill it **in the evening.***
[7] ***And they shall take of the blood, and strike it on the two side posts*** *and on the upper door post of the houses, wherein they shall eat it.*
[8] *And they shall **eat the flesh in that night**, roast with fire, and unleavened bread; and with bitter herbs they shall eat it*
Exodus 12: 1-3, 6-8

What does: *kill it in the evening* (Exodus 12:6) mean? The Hebrew text of Exodus 12:6 is actually *kill it between the evenings*. The *Jewish Encyclopedia* gives the following definition.

The time "between the two evenings" ("ben ha-'arbayim") was construed to mean "after noon and until nightfall"

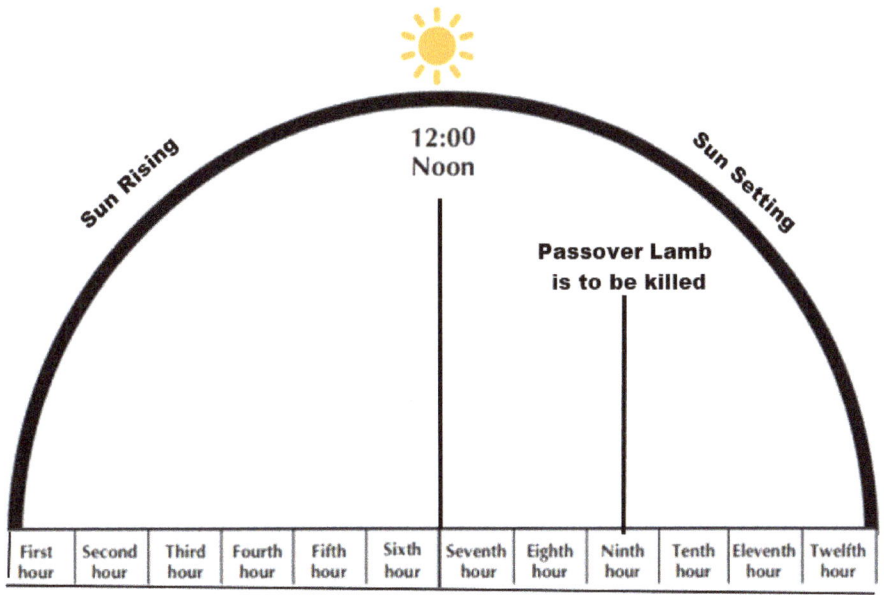

Sunrise is always at 6:00 AM and Sunset is at 6:00 PM. A Jewish day is different from a Western Gregorian day; The Jewish day is a 24-hour period of time that begins at 6:00 PM at sunset. The sun will start to rise at 6:00 AM and reach its zenith at 12:00 noon……. It will then begin its decline until 6:00 PM. Between the two evenings is a Jewish term which corresponds to our three o'clock in the afternoon. Regardless of any disagreement among Jewish Rabbis as to when the Passover Lamb should be killed, it can be easily settled by any Christian. Jesus Christ…...the Lamb of God…was crucified (killed) at 3:00 PM on Nisan 14 (Matthew 27:46, Luke 23:44). The Jewish 9th hour is 3:00 PM - 4:00 PM). Christ, our perfect Passover Lamb without spot or blemish, died at exactly 3:00 PM…. The same time that the High Priest was slaughtering the Passover Lamb for the people in Herod's Temple. The antitype perfectly satisfied the type.

The Passover Lamb was selected on Nisan 10, and kept in the house for a period of 4 days. For 4 days (Nisan 10 – Nisan 11 - Nisan 12 -Nisan 13) it was examined to make sure that it was pure and unblemished. On *Nisan 14* between the evenings, they were instructed to slaughter the lamb and prepare it for the evening meal. The blood was to be caught in a bowl, and smeared over the lintel or over the door of each Hebrew house. The lamb was to be eaten that night, which was actually the first few hours of Nisan 15. Nisan 15 marked the 1st day of the 7-day *Feast of Unleavened Bread which* began at 6:00 PM. At midnight, the *Avenging Angel* of the Lord would pass over every house in Egypt. The firstborn male in any house without blood over the door would be killed, and the firstborn of all livestock outside the house would also be killed (Genesis 12:29).

This was the 10th and final plague that caused the Pharaoh of Egypt to *let the people go* after his firstborn son was slain. The Lamb is to be eaten after Nisan 14, 6:00 PM on Nisan 15. The Passover meal was to commemorate and recall remembrance of this event for perpetual generations. Nisan 15 is the first day of the 7-day Feast of Unleavened Bread. On the night of Nisan 15, 1450 BC every family would gather around the fire where the Lamb was roasted. The entire family was to eat the Passover Lamb. No bones were to be broken and it was to be completely consumed. Following the meal, the remains were to be presented as a *burnt offering* to the Lord. At midnight, the *Death Angel* would *pass over* every house with blood of the Lamb on the lintel of the front door. After midnight, Moses would be summoned by the Pharoah whose firstborn son had been slain. In agony, he commanded Moses and the Children of Israel to *leave Egypt*.

Messianic Application

Jesus Christ arrived in Jerusalem on Nisan 10 and stayed at the house of Lazarus for four days before He was arrested around midnight on Nisan 14. Every day He went to the Temple and was examined and scrutinized by the Sadducees and Pharisees who sought to discredit Him. He was found to be without spot or blemish. He was the antitype of the exodus Passover lamb that was examined for 4 days by every family. On the morning of Nisan, He was taken before Pilate to be sentenced. After an extensive investigation to find fault in Jesus, Pilate said to the chief priests and to the people*: I find no fault in this man* (Luke 23:4). In an act of contempt and hatred, the Jews said: *Free Barrabus the murderer* and *Crucify Him*. The time had come for Jesus Christ the perfect Passover Lamb to die for the sins of the world. Christ completely fulfilled the Feast of Passover when He was crucified on the cross of Calvary.

For even Christ our Passover is sacrificed for us   I Corinthians 5:7

When John was baptizing at the Jordan River in 26 AD, he looked up:

John sees Jesus coming unto him, and said: Behold the Lamb of God, which taketh away the sin of the world   John 1:29

The Hebrew word *Passover* is literally translated *Lamb*, and Christ is God's perfect Passover sacrificial lamb. He was both the sacrifice and the one who offered the sacrifice.

Our Lord Jesus Christ died for our sins at 3:00 PM on Nisan 14, at exactly the same time that the High Priest was killing the Passover Lamb in the temple. At that time the veil that separated the Holy Place from the Holy of Holies was *rent in two* from top to bottom, signifying that the Levitical sacrificial system had ended. The Old Covenant had passed away; the New Covenant had come.

The night before Jesus Christ was crucified, He held a last supper with His beloved apostles and Judas the traitor. The Last Supper is one of the most important and beautiful moments of Jesus Messiah's ministry. It is also one of the most highly debated topics to those who do not fully understand the meaning of that last supper. On the last night of His time on earth, Jesus gathered His 12 apostles to celebrate the Passover. There is an ongoing debate as to exactly what Passover meal Christ was holding. This was Tuesday after 6:00 PM on Nisan 14. Later that night, Christ would be arrested and early the next morning (Wednesday Morning) he would be handed over to the Jews who cried: *Crucify Him! Crucify Him!!*

It is instructive to understand what happened to Jesus Christ in the last few days before His crucifixion.

1. After walking into Jerusalem on Nisan 10, as was His custom He immediately went to the Temple to teach and heal. After spending the day in Jerusalem, He walked to Bethany and spent the night of Nisan 10 (Nisan 11). at the house of His friend Lazarus.
2. This was repeated on Nisan 11 (day and night), Nisan 12 (day and night) and Nisan 13 (day)
3. After spending Nisan 13 (day) in the Temple, things were about to change dramatically.

[3] Then assembled together the chief priests, and the scribes, and the elders of the people, unto the palace of the high priest, who was called Caiaphas,

[4] And consulted that they might take Jesus by subtilty, and kill him

Matthew 26: 3-5

As Nisan 13 ended at 6:00 PM, Nisan 14 began. After leaving His last supper with His 11 disciples (Judas had already left to betray Christ) several prophecies were about to be fulfilled:

(1) He would be arrested in the Garden of Gethsemane on the Mt. of Olives by Roman soldiers

(2) after being beaten and abused, He would be dragged in chains to the Jewish High Priest

(3) After undeserved persecution and inquiry, the High priest took Jesus to an underground dungeon where He spent the night in chains, being ridiculed and spit upon.

(4) Early the next morning (still Nisan 14), Christ is taken before Pilate for sentencing. The High Priest did not have the authority to sentence anyone to death, only Pilate as the Roman Magistrate over Jerusalem could pass a death sentence).

(5) After intense questioning, a strange thing happened. Pilate could find no fault in Jesus Christ. This should have been expected, since Christ was our Perfect Sacrificial Lamb without spot or blemish.

(6) God had a plan since Adam sinned to redeem all men through the death of Jesus Christ. This plan of God would be fulfilled, and so the people demanded that a hardened murderer named Barrabus who was awaiting death by crucifixion be freed and that Christ would take his place. And so it was.... He who was sinless became sin for you and I,

and by His undeserved death forgave the sins of the world....... Past, present and Future. The Old Covenant and the law were finished, and a New Covenant was initiated which offered salvation to Jews and Gentiles alike, based upon *faith*.

This sequence of events as revealed in the Holy Scriptures has been the subject of intense debate. The debate revolves around the following question: Did Christ eat the Passover Meal as required or did He initiate a new ordinance?

[1] *After two days was the feast of the Passover, and of unleavened bread: and the chief priests and the scribes sought how they might take him by craft, and put him to death.*
[2] *But they said: Not on the feast day, lest there be an uproar of the people*   Mark 14: 1-2

This verse is often isolated and misunderstood. It was asked in Bethany at the house of Siman the Leper on the last evening (Wednesday night) that Christ would be a free man (Mark 14: 1-3).

And the first day of unleavened bread, when they killed the Passover, his disciples said unto Him: Where wilt thou that we go and prepare that thou mayest eat the Passover?   Mark 14:12

How should Mark 14:12 be understood from a Jewish standpoint?

First, Mark clearly states that the Passover Lamb was to be killed on *the first day of unleavened bread.* But, the Feast of Unleavened Bread did not begin until after 8:00 PM on Nisan 15. This paradox is easily solved if one understands the nature of Passover in the 1st Century. By 30 AD when Christ was crucified (See Phillips, *The Birth and Death of Jesus Christ*: Phillips, *The Birth of Jesus Christ: a Forensic Analysis*: and Fred R. Coulter, *The Day Jesus Christ Died*) the entire period of time

Between Nisan 14 (Traditional Passover) and Sivan 8 (Feast of Pentecost) had become known as the *Passover Season*, and Nisan 14-Nisan 21) was called the *Feast of Unleavened Bread*. Mark was writing to the Jews who used this 1st century practice.

Matthew also wrote that:

*Now the **first day of the feast of unleavened bread** the disciples came to Jesus, saying unto him: Where wilt thou that we prepare for thee to eat the Passover?*   Matthew 26:17

Mattew did not include Nisan 14 as part of Passover meal, but (incorrectly) included Nisan 14 as part of the Feast of Unleavened Bread.

[1] *Now **before the Feast of the Passover**, when Jesus knew that his hour was come that he should depart out of this world unto the Father, having loved his own which were in the world, he loved them unto the end.*
[2] *And supper being ended, the devil having now put into the heart of Judas Iscariot, Simon's son, to betray him*   John 13: 1-2

John never mentioned the Feast of Unleavened Bread, but specifically wrote that the Passover meal of Christ on the night of Nisan 14 was before the usual Feast of Passover. In Leviticus 23, God commanded that the Passover Lamb be killed at 3:00 PM on Nisan 14, and that the Feast of Unleavened Bread would be held Nisan 15-Nisan 21 (Leviticus 23: 5-6, Exodus 12:6). By the 1st century AD…..specifically 30 AD when Christ was crucified…… the Jews had begun to call Passover every day between Nisan 14 when the Passover Lamb was to be slain, and Nisan 15-Nisan 21 which was the Feast of Unleavened Bread. Jesus Christ, as was His custom during Nisan 10-Nisan 13, taught and healed in the Temple all day on Nisan 13 until it closed at 6:00 PM (the start of Nisan 14).

Christ knew that he would be arrested around midnight on Nisan 14; sentenced to die by Crucifixion on the morning of Nisan 14; nailed to the cross at 9:00 AM on Nisan 14; die at 3:00 PM on Nisan 14; and be placed in the tomb before 6:00 PM on Nisan 14. Jesus Christ *knew* that He would be dead and in the tomb before the Passover meal was to be eaten the night of Nisan 15. The Lords last Supper was with His apostles during the early night hours of Nisan 14…. probably between 8:00 PM and 10:00 PM (He was arrested in the Garden of Gethsemane on the Mount of Olives around midnight).

This question (Mark 14:12) of where should the Passover Meal should be eaten took place just after 6:00 PM on Nisan 14, which by the 1st Century BC was (incorrectly) called Passover and a part of the Feast of Unleavened Bread. The apostles understood that Christ must be Crucified and die on the afternoon of Nisan 14, less than 21 hours later (Matthew 26: 21-22). Christ *knew* that He would be in the grave before the night of Nisan 15…….it is ridiculous to believe anything else. Christ desired to eat his last evening meal on the night of Nisan 14 with His beloved disciples. He also used this occasion to instruct all Christians (body of Christ) to remember Him by observing what we now call *communion*. This was *His* Passover meal which was to be observed by all Christians. In Luke 22: 15-16 Christ said:

*And he said unto them: With desire I have desired to **eat this passover** with you **before I suffer**:*   Luke 22:15

Christ instituted the Lord's Last Supper for two reasons: (1) He desired to meet with all of His apostles before he would be arrested (2) He wanted to clearly explain that He would die later that same day (3) His death Wednesday afternoon at 3:00 PM finished the law and the entire Levitical sacrificial system, but the Jews were still commanded to observe a Jewish Passover meal every year on Nisan 15. Recall that its original intent was to remember how God had rescued them from Egyptian slavery. (4) Whether or not a Christian celebrates Passover would be a matter of conscience for the individual Christian. Like all the Old Testament Spring Jewish Feasts, the Passover meal was to be observed forever to remember how the Lord rescued them from Egyptian slavery. There is a great deal of confusion by Christians today surrounding His command to observe Passover and the Passover meal forever. Christians today are not required to observe the Passover or the Passover Seder (meal). This is a Jewish meal. Today, we (Christians) are to celebrate the Lords Last supper *as often as we will* to remember Christ's atoning work on the cross.

Christians are not bound to observe Passover every year as God commanded Israel, but they should not look down upon another believer who does or does not observe the Passover or other special Jewish days and feasts. Paul told us:

Let no one judge you in food or in drink, or regarding a festival or a new moon or Sabbaths, which are a shadow of things to come, but the substance is of Christ Colossians 2:16-17

Some Christians do celebrate Passover as the Jews celebrate it. They eat roasted lamb, bitter herbs, and unleavened matzo. Others follow the instructions that Jesus gave to his disciples at the Last Supper before he was crucified, and share bread and wine instead of roasted lamb. The Lords Last Supper is held in almost every Christian church once a month. This is somewhat misunderstood since it is called *communion* and is a required church ordinance. Jesus Christ said:

And he took bread, and when he had given thanks, he broke it and gave it to them, saying: This is my body, which is given for you. **Do this in remembrance of me**. *And likewise, the cup after they had eaten,* *saying: This cup that is poured out for you is the new covenant in my blood*   Luke 22: 19-20

[53] *Then Jesus said unto them, Verily, verily, I say unto you: Except ye eat the flesh of the Son of man, and drink his blood, ye have no life in you.*
[54] *Whoso eats my flesh, and drinks my blood, hath eternal life; and I will raise him up at the last day*   John 6: 53-54

[26] *And as they were eating, Jesus took bread, and blessed it, and brake it, and gave it to the disciples, and said, Take, eat; this is my body.*
[27] *And he took the cup, and gave thanks, and gave it to them, saying, Drink ye all of it;*
[28] *For* **this is my blood of the New Testament** (Covenant), *which is shed for many for the remission of sins.*   Matthew 26: 26-28

It is right and correct that the Lords Sacrificial death be remembered in church when communion is given. But one must be careful that a required church ordinance becomes a ritualistic exercise. God warned the Jews of just this very thing.

Bring no more vain oblations; incense is an abomination unto me; the new moons and sabbaths, the calling of assemblies, I cannot away with; it is iniquity, even the solemn meeting   Isaiah 1:13

When one receives communion in church today, it generally follows the guidelines of the Catholic church. It must be served by special people…. specially prepared or in packaged or pre-prepared portions…with age-old ritualistic presentation. Never forget that this is a very personal experience, and should be done with love and thanksgiving. *Do this in remembrance of me*…. This means often with your children and family at home.

Today, some Christians have twisted the meaning of Scripture to accommodate their own personal pleasure. Some Bible studies have become more about a time of *fellowship* than about serious Bible study, reverent prayer, and a desire to please God. Evangelism has become optional and turned into friendship time where we go to eat breakfast or lunch. Often the gospel is never presented because Christians become more interested in personal relationships. Some professing Christians attend church when it is convenient, and stay home to watch the Super Bowl. Some church attenders are just like those in Sodom and Gomorrah. It is estimated that almost sixty-six percent of men and thirty-three percent of women who attend church watch pornography.

[47] *Verily, verily, I say unto you, He that believeth on me hath everlasting life.*
[48] *I am that bread of life.*   John 3: 47-48

Feast of Unleavened Bread (Nisan 15-21**)**
The Feast of Unleavened Bread is a memorial to when the Children of Israel left Egypt in haste on Nisan 15. The Feast of Unleavened Bread starts at 6:00 PM on Nisan 14 and continues for seven full days until 6:00 PM on Nisan 21. It is important to note that both Nisan 15 and Nisan 21 were designated as *High Sabbath days*. During these 7 days there was to be no unleavened bread in any household. No servile work was to be done on either Nisan 15 or Nisan 21, and if food is to be consumed it must be prepared by the family in their house. The Exodus from Egypt was sudden. In Exodus 12 we are told:

So the people took their dough before it was leavened, having their kneading bowls bound and in their clothes on their shoulders
Exodus 12:34

There was to be no leavened bread at all in any household for seven days. All leaven was to be removed by 6:00 PM on Nisan 14. This was serious business.

For seven days no leaven shall be found in your houses, since whoever eats what is leavened, that same person shall be **cut off from the**

congregation of Israel, *whether he is a stranger or a native of the land.* Exodus 12:19

In Exodus 16:2, the Israelites complained that they had no food, so God miraculously provided *manna* to them every day. The manna was picked every morning on Sunday-Friday. The manna picked on Sunday-Thursday only lasted one day; the manna picked on Friday morning lasted two days and then spoiled on the third day to honor the Jewish Sabbath (Saturday). Aaron the High Priest put a *pot of manna* into the Ark of the Covenant; it *never* spoiled.

The Feast of Unleavened Bread was not observed until the Jordan River was crossed, the land was conquered, the land had been divided into 12 portions and the people started to grow their own crops.
The evening of Nisan 14 (Nisan 15) was a weekly Sabbath Day called a *High Sabbath*. It was just as holy as any normal (Saturday) Sabbath day. Nisan 15 was the 1st day of the 7-day *Feast of Unleavened Bread* which lasted 7 days and ended at 6:00 PM on Nisan 17. Nisan 17 was also designated as a *High Sabbath Day*.

Selection and preparation of the Passover Lamb was not the only critical activity which took place immediately before the Feast of Unleavened Bread. The days immediately preceding Nisan 15 was a time during which all Leavened Bread had to be removed from the house…...Every morsel, crumb and piece of Unleavened Bread was to be found and removed. In fact, all leaven had to be removed also. This search intensified during the days of Nisan 1-Nisan 14. This is still done today by every Jewish family, and it is to remind the Nation of Israel that they had to immediately leave Egypt on Nisan 15…… So quickly that there was no time to prepare and bake leavened bread.

The beginning of the Feast of Unleavened Bread on Nisan 15 was marked by the Passover Supper, but what about the last day of the feast on Nisan 21? This is not clear, but it is conjectured that this date coincided with the day on which God gave each person in the exodus a bread called *manna*. Incredible as it may seem, the Children of Israel were continually complaining about something. As they fled Egypt, the people cried out: *Why have you (Moses) led us out of Egypt to a wilderness where there is no bread to eat?* God heard their cries (complaints) and He caused a strange bread to appear on the ground every night (Manna is Hebrew for *what is it?*). The Israelites were instructed to gather all the bread they could eat in one day each morning in baskets. After 24 hours, the bread would spoil and could not be eaten. On Friday morning, God instructed them to gather enough Manna to last Friday and Saturday (Saturday was the Jewish Sabbath day).

Note that the 7 Feasts of Israel were to be observed forever, but they would not begin to be observed until the Nation of Israel settled in the *Promised Land of Canaan*, north of the River Jordan. The Israelites were not hunter-gatherers, but they were farmers and an agricultural nation who worked the land. The main crop was *wheat*, which was planted in the Fall and began to mature in the Spring. The crops that sustained the Nation of Israel were nurtured by God. Their proper maturity and growth depended upon the *early and latter rains.* As the crops sprung from the seed and began to grow, the field became a mixture of *Barley* and *Wheat*. The barley was heartier than wheat and would mature months before the precious wheat. Hence, the 1st grain harvest was barley and the 2nd was wheat. Barley was inferior to wheat, but it could still be used to make bread and flower. The Feast of Firstfruits was to offer a *wavesheath* of barley to God and solicit his blessing on the current Barley crop. The wheat was a better grain crop, but it would mature much slower than the heartier, faster growing barley.
Selection and preparation of the Passover Lamb was not the only critical activity which took place immediately before the Feast of Unleavened Bread. The days immediately preceding Nisan 15 was a time during which all Leavened Bread had to be removed from the house……Every

morsel, crumb and piece of Unleavened Bread was to be found and removed. In fact, all leaven had to be removed also. This search intensified during the days of Nisan 1-Nisan 14. This is still done today by every Jewish family, and it is to remind the Nation of Israel that they had to immediately leave Egypt on Nisan 15…… So quickly that there was no time to prepare and bake leavened bread.

The Feast of Unleavened Bread is a memorial to when the Children of Israel left Egypt in haste after eating the Passover Lamb the evening of Nisan 14, which was the night portion of Nisan 15. It was such a hasty departure, that the women had no time to prepare leavened bread. The Feast of Unleavened Bread started at 6:00 PM on Wednesday and continued for seven full days until 6:00 pm on Nisan 21. It is important to note that both Nisan 15 and Nisan 21 were designated as a *High Sabbath*. It was just as holy as any normal Jewish Sabbath Day (Saturday). During the Feast of Unleavened Bread, there was to be no leaven in the prescence of each Israelite. No servile work was to be done on these days, and if bread was to be cooked and consumed it must be prepared with no leaven. Leaven was symbolic of sin, and there could be trace of sin during the Exodus from Egypt. In Exodus 12 we are told: *So, the people took their dough before it was leavened, having their kneading bowls bound and in their clothes on their shoulders* (Exodus 12:34). When the Feast of Unleavened Bread was observed in subsequent years, starting with Nisan 15, there was to be no leavened bread at all in any household for Seven days. All leaven was to be removed on or before Nisan 14. This was serious business.

For Seven days no leaven shall be found in your houses, since **whoever eats what is leavened, that same person shall be cut off from the congregation of Israel**, *whether he is a stranger or a native of the land* Exodus 12:19

In Exodus 16:2, the Israelites complained that they had no food, so God miraculously provided *manna* (What is it? in Hebrew) to them every day. The manna was picked in the mornings of Sunday-Friday. The manna only lasted one day; the manna picked on Friday morning lasted two days and then spoiled on the third day to honor the Jewish Sabbath (Saturday). Moses put a *pot of manna* into the Ark of the Covenant and it *never* spoiled. The Feast of Unleavened bread was not instituted until the Children of Israel crossed the Jordan River, conquered their enemies and became an agricultural society.

Messianic Application
In the scriptures, *leaven* is representative of *sin*. Our Lord Jesus Christ fulfilled all of the law. His life was perfect in every way. He was the unleavened, sinless bread from heaven. Since He was sinless, He was without *spot or blemish*. He was resurrected and lifted up to God, and He was an acceptable and perfect sacrifice to God.

[6] *Your glorying is not good. Know ye not that a little leaven will leaven the whole lump?*
[7] *Purge out therefore the old leaven, that ye may be a new lump, as ye are unleavened. For even Christ our Passover is sacrificed for us*
I Corinthians 5: 6-7

At the Lord's Last Supper, our Lord Jesus Christ said that He was the Bread which fulfilled the feast.

And as they did eat, Jesus took bread, and blessed, and brake it, and gave to them, and said, Take, eat: this is my body. Mark 14:22

And Jesus said unto them, I am the bread of life: he that cometh to me shall never hunger; and he that believeth on me shall never thirst.
John 6:35

I am the bread of life. He who comes to me shall never hunger.
John 6:35

He was also the *manna that never spoiled*, eternally perfect.

[51] *I am the living bread which came down from heaven: if any man eats of this bread, he shall live forever: and the bread that I will give is my flesh, which I will give for the life of the world.*
[58] *This is that bread which came down from heaven: not as your fathers did eat manna, and are dead: he that eats of this bread shall live forever.*   John 6: 51, 58

Christ was nailed to the Cross of Calvary on Nisan 14 at 9:00 AM. He *gave up the ghost* and died at 3:00 PM, at exactly the same time that the High Priest in Herod's Temple slaughtered the Passover Lamb. Jesus was buried before 6:00 PM, and He became the perfect Passover lamb of God. Jesus was our perfect Passover Lamb, without spot or blemish. He was also the eternal *bread of life* which was placed in the Ark of the Covenant.

The Jews fail to recognize that Jesus Christ is the eternal, perfect Passover Lamb. It was the Blood the Lamb (Exodus 12: 6-7) which resulted in the Angel of death passing over every Jewish house, but this was clearly just a type of the sacrificial death and shedding of blood on the Cross of calvary which was responsible for the Jews being passed over (John 1:29, I Corinthians 5: 7-8, I Peter 1: 18-20). Does this mean that Jews and Gentiles alike are now required to eat what is now the Passover Seder? This is a point of confusion to many Christians today. Recall that the 7 Feasts were to be held by the Jews each year to commemorate and remember how God freed them from Egyptian Slavery. These feasts were all to be perpetual. Hence, every Jew is requited to hold them in remembrance. Gentile Christians were not a part of the Exodus, and they are not required to hold any of the feasts of Israel on a yearly basis. All Jews today still hold a Passover Seder on Nisan 15. This is a fascinating ceremony, and while the Jews may not completely comprehend the ritual, every component of the Passover Seder is a type of something which was accomplished by our Lord Jesus Christ. It is not necessary for any Christian (unless that Person is a Jew) to observe the Passover Meal on Nisan 15.

Leavened bread is always a type of corruption, and leaven a type of sin. Just a small amount will leaven a whole loaf of bread. Unleavened bread is a type of holiness, purity and sinlessness. The entire life of Jesus Christ and His sacrificial death was *unleavened. He suffered death just like a grain of wheat does when it is picked from the stalk, but death could not hold him in the grave.* He was the perfect sacrificial Lamb of God without spot or blemish. After He tasted physical death, He did not suffer the natural process of corruption. His body did not return to dust which was the fate of Adam, Eve and every other human who would remain in the grave for an extended period of time (Genesis. 3:19; Psalms 16:10). The power of death was destroyed after only 3 days and 3 nights in the grave. Why did Christ have to endure death for 3 days and 3 nights anyway? *First*, He used that period of time to descend into Paradise and announce to all those Jews who had died in the faith of Abraham that their long-awaited Messiah had arrived. *Second*, His sacrificial death and resurrection was for Jews and Gentiles alike, and the 1st century Jew had a custom that a person was not confirmed dead until after 3 days and 3 nights had elapsed. This is why Jesus waited for over 3 days to raise His good friend Lazarus.

While this is certainly one application, I think it is equally important to recall that unleavened bread is called the *bread of affliction (lechem oni)*. Does this mean that we are supposed to *afflict or burden* ourselves as we serve Jesus Chrisy? Often it seems so, but it really means to humbly *identify* with the meekness and humility that Jesus Christ endured to reconcile us to Hm and his Father. Isaiah wrote about the Messiah as a Suffering Servant:

[5] *But he was wounded for our transgressions, he was bruised for our iniquities: the chastisement of our peace was upon him; and with his stripes we are healed.*
[6] *All we like sheep have gone astray; we have turned everyone to his own way; and the LORD hath laid on him the iniquity of us all.*
[7] *He was oppressed, and he was afflicted, yet he opened not his mouth:*

he is brought as a lamb to the slaughter, and as a sheep before her shearers is dumb, so he opened not his mouth.   Isaiah 53: 5-7

Yeshua warned us about the *leaven* (corrupting influence) of the Pharisees and the Sadducees -- and even of the politicians of his day (Matthew 16: 6-12; Mark 8:15). leaven is also *hypocrisy* (ὑπόκρισις): *Beware of the leaven of the Pharisees, which is hypocrisy* (Luke 12:1). But what is hypocrisy? The word is formed from the Greek prefix ὑπὸ (under) combined with the verb κρίνω (to judge), and hence refers to genuine conviction. It is a state of being double minded and insincere. The word can also mean: putting on a show, feigning righteousness or acting with insincerity. The Pharisees, Sadducees and religious leaders during the ministry of Christ only judged Christ as a threat to their control and leadership. Hypocrisy is therefore a form of *self-deception*. It is institutionalized prejudice dressed up as religion; it is counterfeit thinking that hides the truth.

   Modified with all humility and gratefulness from John J. Parsons…https://www.hebrew4christians.com/Holidays/SpringHolidays/Unleavened_Bread/Anavah/anavah.html

The Feast of Firstfruits
The Jewish Feast of Firstfruits is seldom understood and taught by Christians today. This is unfortunate, because we will later show that it holds the key to unlocking the date, day and possibly the year which Christ was crucified. Recall that the evening of Nisan 14 (Nisan 15) was a special Sabbath Day called a *High Sabbath*. There are 7 days in a Hebrew year which have been designated as High Sabbath Days:

   The 1ˢᵗ and 7ᵗʰ days of the *Feast of Unleavened Bread*
                                                                          Leviticus 23: 7-8
  Feast of Pentecost (Shavuot)   Leviticus 23 :15-21
  The Feast of Trumpets (Rosh Hashanah)   Leviticus 23: 23-25
  The Feast of Yom Kippur (Day of Atonement)   Leviticus 23: 26-32

The 1st and 8th days of the *Feast of Tabernacles* (Sukkoth)
Leviticus 23: 33-36

These 7 days are just as holy as any normal (Saturday) Sabbath day. Nisan 15 was the 1st day of the 7-day *Feast of Unleavened Bread* which lasted 7 days and ended at 6:00 PM on Nisan 21. Both Nisan 15 and Nisan 21 were designated as a *High Sabbath Day*. The beginning of the Feast of Unleavened Bread on Nisan 15 was marked by the Passover Supper, but what special event happened on the last day of the 7-day feast on Nisan 21? This is not clear, but it is conjectured that this date coincided with the day on which God gave each person in the exodus bread called *manna*.

Incredible as it may seem, the Children of Israel were continually complaining about something. As they fled Egypt, the people cried out: *Why have you (Moses) led us out of Egypt to a wilderness where there is no bread to eat?* God heard their cries (complaints) and He caused a strange bread to appear on the ground every night (*Manna* is Hebrew for *what is it?*). The Israelites were instructed to gather all the bread they could eat in one day each morning in baskets. After 24 hours, the bread would spoil and could not be eaten. On Friday morning, God instructed them to gather enough Manna to last Friday and Saturday (Saturday was the weekly Jewish Sabbath day).

The 7 Feasts of Israel were to be observed forever (Leviticus 23), but the *Feast of Firstfruits* would not be observed until the Nation of Israel settled in the *Promised Land of Canaan*, north of the River Jordan. The Israelites were not hunter-gatherers, but they were farmers and an agricultural nation who worked the land. The main crop was *wheat*, which was planted in the Fall and began to mature in late Spring. The crops that sustained the Nation of Israel were nurtured by God. Their proper maturity and growth depended upon the *early and latter rains.* As the crops sprung from the seed and began to grow, the field became a mixture of *Barley* and *Wheat*. The barley was heartier than wheat and would mature months before the precious wheat. Hence, the 1st grain harvest was barley and the 2nd was wheat. Barley was inferior to wheat, but it could still be used to make bread and flower. The Feast of Firstfruits was to offer a *wavesheath* of *barley* to God and ask his blessing on the current Barley crop. The wheat was a better grain crop, but it would mature much slower than the heartier, faster growing barley.

The *Feast of Firstfruits* is one of the 7 Holy Feasts of Israel, and is equally important to both Jews and Gentiles. The Feast of Firstfruits is the 3rd feast of Israel in the Spring months (Passover-Unleavened Bread Firstfruits), but it is intimately connected to the Feast of Unleavened Bread. It is to be observed on the only Sunday which falls within the 7-day Feast of Unleavened Bread (Nisan 15–Nisan 21). In order to understand the relationship between the Feast of Firstfruits, The Feast of Unleavened Bread and the Feast of Pentecost, it is necessary to review the ancient Jewish Lunar Calendar.

The Jewish year is divided into two parts: Spring and Fall. Nisan 1 initiates the Spring, and Tishri 1 initiates the Fall. Nisan 1 is considered to be the 1st day of the Jewish *Religious year* and it will wander over two Gregorian months of March and April. The Jewish month of Tishri 1 is considered to be the beginning of the Jewish *Civil year* and will wander between two Gregorian months of September and October. The Jewish year is called a *Lunar year* because each month begins on a New Moon. The Gregorian year is a *Solar Year*, and it is based upon the amount of time it takes the earth to make a complete revolution around the sun. A Gregorian Solar year is 365 days long except in a leap year which is 366 days long. The Jewish calendar year will vary between 353, 354, 355, 383, 384, or 385 days long. The length of a Jewish calendar year varies between 353 and 385 days in order to have the 1st day of every month coincide as close as possible with a new moon. The Jewish calendar is remarkable accurate over a period of 19 years. Every 19 years the length of each month will average 365.25 days, and the Jewish calendar will sync with the Gregorian Calendar. This 19-year period of time is called a *Metonic Cycle*.

It is often necessary for NASA and other space research organizations to equate the date of a Gregorian year to the corresponding date of a Jewish calendar year. To accomplish this goal, computer scientists have written several complex computer programs to do just that across thousands of future and past years. Almost all theologians agree that Jesus Christ died between the years of 29 AD and 34 AD. The following table shows the Gregorian Calendar date and the day of Nisan 14 between 29 AD and 34 AD using two reliable and accurate calendar convertors. Both produce the same results (*Fourmilab calendar converter* and the *Abdicate Calendar Convertor*).

In two previous theological investigations, it has been shown that the year that Christ died was 30 AD (Phillips, *The Life and Death of Christ*:

Day	Gregorian Calendar Date
Sat	April 14, 29 AD
Wed	April 3, 30 AD
Mon	Mar 24, 31 AD
Mon	April 12, 32 AD
Sun	April 3, 33 AD
Mon	March 20, 34 AD

Phillips, *The Birth and Death of Jesus Christ: a Forensic Analysis*). This was also shown to be true by Coulter, *The Day That Jesus the Christ Died*). We will prove that Jesus Christ had to be crucified on Nisan 14,

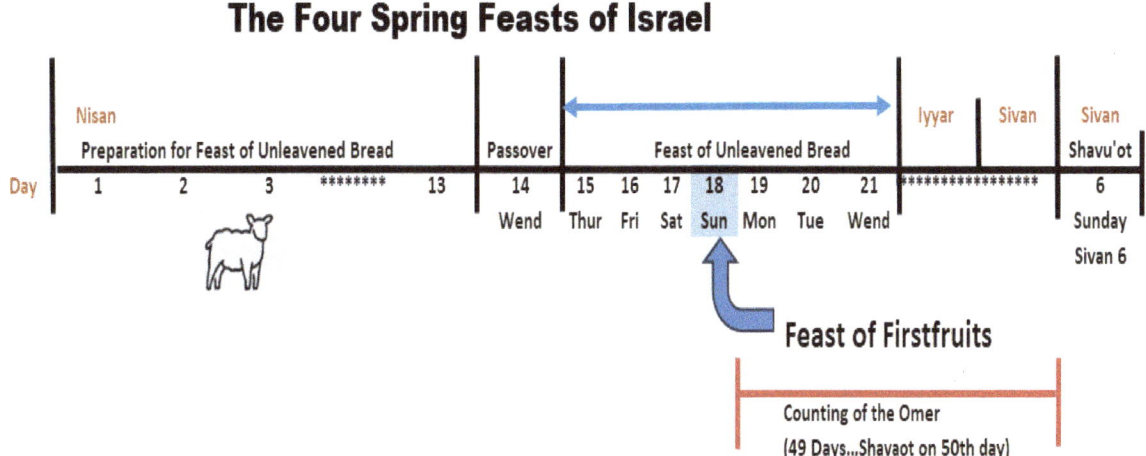

30 to spend a full 3 days and 3 nights in the grave. A timeline for 30 AD is shown below for the Four Spring Feasts of Israel.

Nisan is the month that the Children of Israel began their journey from Egypt after God had rescued them from over 200 years of slavery. Moses was chosen by God to lead the Nation of Israel out of Egypt starting on Nisan 15. Prior to the Exodus, the 1st month of the Hebrew year was designated as Tishri. After the exodus began, God commanded that the 1st month of every Hebrew year would be the Month of Nisan.

[1] *And the LORD spoke unto Moses and Aaron in the land of Egypt, saying,*
[2] *This month shall be unto you the beginning of months: it shall be the first month of the year to you*   Exodus 12: 1-2

The first of the 7 yearly Jewish Feasts was called the *Feast of Passover*, but it was not a Feast at all. It was the day on which the Passover Lamb was to be killed and preparations made for the *Feast of Unleavened Bread* on Nisan15. The Passover Lamb was to remain in each Jewish household for 4 days and 4 nights. It became a pet, and the entire family grieved when it was slain on the afternoon of Nisan 14. The blood of the Lamb was to be caught in an urn, and as the night of Nisan 15 approached it was to be spread on the lintel of the front door in preparation for a strange and horrible plague. At midnight, God would send to every household in Egypt an *Angel of Death*. As the angel passed over each house, if blood was found on the front entrance the Angel would *pass over* that house. If the blood of God's covenant was not found, the *firstborn* of every animal and the youngest child of each family would be killed. It was this unspeakable act that finally caused the Pharoah of Egypt to *let the Israelites go.*

The lamb was too be eaten on the night of Nisan 15, and it was to commemorate the night when the Egyptian Pharoah finally gave the command to *let the Children of Israel go.* It was also on this night that the *Angel of Death* visited or *passed over* every household in Egypt. God had sent this angel to every household (Jews and Egyptians) with instructions to kill every firstborn child and animal in Egypt. The Jews were commanded to slaughter a lamb on the afternoon of Nisan 14 and then to prepare it for the Passover supper on the night of Nisan 15. The blood of the Passover Lamb was to be collected and then smeared upon the lintel (door trim) of each house. If the *Angel of Death* came to a house which had blood protection, he would "Pass over" that house and the firstborn would be spared. Since the night of all Jewish days began at 6:00 PM, this was called a *night to be much remembered* (Exodus 12:42). The Pharoh's arrogance and pride would result in his firstborn son being slain by the Death Angel. This was the plague brought upon Egypt by God which finally resulted in the liberation of God's people. The Feast of Passover was ordained by God in perpetuity to be remembered and observed.

The Feast of Firstfruits was the time when the grain crop of Barley was to be dedicated to the Lord as a wavesheath offering by the High Priest in the Temple. It was to be held at sunrise on the Sunday that immediately followed the only Jewish Sabbath Day (Saturday) during the 7-day Feast of Unleavened Bread. After the Jewish weekly sabbath day of Saturday ended at 6:00 PM, the High Priest and several other priests would visit a chosen field in which the barley was growing. Stalks (bundle) of Barley would be picked and bundled into a sheath. The sheath of barley would then be taken to the Temple and placed on the altar. The barley would remain there overnight, and early the next morning it would be waved before the Lord. No barley could be picked, used, bought or sold before the Lord had placed His approval and blessings upon the new grain crop.

The specific instructions of when the Feast of Firstfruits……now called Easter Sunday…... was to be observed every year.

[10] Speak unto the children of Israel, and say unto them, When ye be come into the land which I give unto you, and shall reap the harvest thereof, then ye shall bring a sheaf of the Firstfruits of your harvest unto the priest:
[11] And he shall wave the sheaf before the LORD, to be accepted for you: on the morrow after the sabbath the priest shall wave it.
[12] And ye shall offer that day when ye wave the sheaf and a he lamb without blemish of the first year as a burnt offering unto the LORD.
[13] And the meat offering thereof shall be two tenth deals of fine flour mingled with oil, an offering made by fire unto the LORD for a sweet savor: and the drink offering thereof shall be of wine, the fourth part of an hin.
[14] And ye shall eat neither bread, nor parched corn, nor green ears, until the selfsame day that ye have brought an offering unto your God: it shall be a statute forever throughout your generations in all your dwellings.
[15] And ye shall count unto you from the morrow after the sabbath, from the day that ye brought the sheaf of the wave offering; seven sabbaths shall be complete:
[16] Even unto the morrow after the seventh sabbath shall ye number fifty days; and ye shall offer a new meat offering unto the LORD
Leviticus 23: 10-16

The Feast of Firstfruits starts on the *morrow after the Sabbath*. There was a raging battle between the Pharisees and the Sadducees as to what this means. The first day of the Feast of Unleavened Bread (Nisan 15) was a *Sabbath*, a *High Sabbath*. The *Sadducees* held that the 50-day count to Pentecost began on Nisan 16 every year, while the *Pharisees* maintained that it started on the day after the *weekly Sabbath* (Saturday).

The above passage says that *Seven Sabbaths must be complete* in the 50-day period. This is Seven complete weeks starting on a Sunday and ending on a Saturday. The 50th day should always be a Sunday. The Jews sometimes call the Feast of Pentecost the *Feast of Weeks*. The term Feast of Weeks is not quite correct. It is not a feast at all, but actually refers to the 7 complete Sabbath cycles (49 days) that take place between the *Feast of Firstfruits* and the *Feast of Pentecost* on the 50th day. This will happen every year if the feast starts on the Sunday following the only Sabbath (Saturday) of Unleavened Bread. We will discuss the Feast of Pentecost next, and it will be proved that the Pharisees were correct.

The 1st Century Catholic Church has renamed the Feast of Firstfruits *Easter*. Easter actually originated as an ancient pagan celebration of the spring equinox. In modern Christianity, the day is dedicated to observing the resurrection of Jesus Christ. However, as the Gospel of Christ spread, early Christians who did not participate in Jewish customs eventually merged their ceremonies with a pagan spring festival, recognizing Easter as resurrection day. One of the most popular symbols associated with Easter is the *Easter egg*. This symbol goes back to the Ancient Babylonians. They believed an egg fell from heaven into the Euphrates River, and "hatched" the goddess of fertility, Astarte (also known as Ashtur, Ishtar, and also Easter). Pagans exchanged eggs as gifts during their springtime festival to celebrate fertility and the ability of women to bring forth life. Today, eggs are painted in bright colors and used in the ever-popular Easter egg hunt, where they are hidden for children to find and collect Another popular Easter symbol is the *Easter bunny*. Like eggs, rabbits represent reproduction and fertility. The Easter Rabbit as symbol of Easter originated in the pagan festival of *Eostre*, represented by a northern goddess whose symbol was a rabbit. There is little about Easter that is celebrated today that originated in the death and resurrection of Jesus Christ. Christ rose from the grave after 3 days and 3 nights on Saturday, Nisan 17 just at 6:00 Pm as Saturday was changing into Sunday. Sunday morning, Christ ascended into heaven as the First fruit of all who would be resurrected later. Easter should be called Firstfruits. Having said that, it is proper that the resurrection of Jesus Christ should be celebrated by Christians today: Just understand where Easter originated and was corrupted into what we call aster today.

Easter should be observed on the only Sunday that falls during the 7-day Feast of Unleavened Bread. Instead, Easter today is observed on the first Sunday after the *Paschal Full Moon*. What is the Paschal Full Moon? This is the first Sunday following the full Moon that occurs on or after the *spring equinox*. Easter is not observed on the same Sunday every year. On the Gregorian calendar, it is always observed on a Sunday between March 22 and April 25. However, Easter is observed between April 4 and May 8 by the Catholic Eastern Orthodox Church.

Messianic Application

It will shortly be shown that the Pharisees count to Pentecost is correct and the count adopted by both the Sadducees and the Catholic Church is incorrect. The real key to determining which religious group was correct is in the spiritual fulfillment of this feast by Jesus Christ. Christ rose early on a Sunday after spending 3 days and 3 nights in the grave, and he is the *Firstfruits* of all who would accept Him as Lord and Savior and be resurrected at what we call the *Rapture*. The Feast of Firstfruits must be on Sunday to satisfy typology. It takes place on Sunday morning in the temple. During the 3.5-year ministry of Jesus Christ, the Feasts of Passover, Unleavened Bread, Firstfruits and Pentecost were considered to be one long feast season which was generally referred to as the *Passover Season*. It was not uncommon in 1 AD to refer to all three as simply *Passover*. The Feast of Firstfruits signified the early maturation of the *barley* crop and the beginning of a long growing season for *wheat*. The Feast of Firstfruits was ritually observed by all Jews throughout the temple eras. When Herod's Temple was destroyed in 70 AD, there was no high priest or temple to continue this ceremony. The *Firstfruit Offerings* were to both please God and to support the Levitical priesthood (Leviticus 23:10-17, Exodus 23:19, Deuteronomy 26:1-11). On the day following the weekly Sabbath of Saturday, as soon as possible after 6:00 PM (Sunday) a *sheaf of barley*, which was an *Omer* (about 2 quarts), was picked from a predetermined location, bound in a sheath and stored in the temple. The next morning at daybreak, the High Priest would wave the sheath of Barley before the Lord. No grain could be harvested, eaten or sold until this was done.

Christ was crucified on Nisan 14. He *gave up the ghost* and died at 3:00 pm, at exactly the same time that the High Priest in Herod's Temple slaughtered the Passover lamb for the burnt sacrifice. Jesus was hastily placed in the tomb of Joseph of Arimathea. This was because 6:00 PM began Nisan 15, and Nisan 15 was a High Holy Day. Anyone crucified during any day preceding a Sabbath Day (Saturday or a Special Sabbath day) had to be removed from the cross and placed in the grave before the Sabbath Day started at 6:00 PM. Jesus was our perfect Passover Lamb, without spot or blemish. He was also the perfect *Bread of Life*, without leaven (sin). He was the final and ultimate Firstfruits offering in 1 AD.

Finally, Jesus Christ was sacrificed for the sins of the world…. Past, present and future. His precious blood was spilled on every individual who would ever live. Sin was no longer the issue. Salvation is now based upon *faith* and *grace*……offered to Jews and Gentiles alike.

The Firstfruits sheaf of Barley was symbolic of the greater *wheat harvest* to come. If the Firstfruit was holy, then the entire harvest would be holy unto the Lord. Paul confirmed the spiritual intent of the Firstfruit offering, and directly related it to the *root* (Israel) and the *branches* (the Body of Christ).

For if the Firstfruit be holy, the lump is also holy: and if the root be holy, so are the branches   Romans 11:16

The Firstfruit offering consecrated the entire harvest to the Lord. It was an *earnest offering* or a *pledge* of the full harvest which was yet to come. As previously explained, this ritual was very important, because no barley from the field could be picked or eaten until the ceremony was completed. In fact, ancient tradition held that on Nisan 1 the High Priest would inspect the *barley in the ear*. The word Nisan actually means *green ear*. If the crop had not matured enough by Nisan 1 to pick a *wave sheaf* on Nisan 15, then an extra month of 29/30 days called *Adar II* would be immediately added to the previous year. While not exact, this was elegant in its simplicity. Periodic insertion of an extra month kept the Jewish lunar-based calendar from getting very far *out of sync* with the solar calendar and the agricultural seasons.

The first of the Firstfruits of thy land thou shalt bring unto the house of the LORD thy God   Exodus 34:26

How beautiful and prophetic was the Firstfruit offering! Christ is everywhere present in the typology. The offering was to be made of *green ears* of corn that would be dried in the fire. Was not our Lord Jesus Christ *tried as if in the fire* by the Pharisees and Sadducees? Was He not tempted at every turn just as we are today? After being offered to the Lord, the dried corn was then to be *beaten* out of the ear for food for the Levites. Was not our Lord Jesus Christ *beaten and bruised* for our sins, and then accepted by God as the Firstfruit offering? *Oil* was also to be poured over the Firstfruits offering; Did not Jesus pour out the *oil* of the Holy Spirit on the day of Pentecost?

Today the Feast of Firstfruits is observed by Christians and is called *Easter*. It is appropriate that Christians observe the resurrection of our risen Savior, but the modern observance called *Easter* has been corrupted. The modern observance of Easter was initiated by the Roman Catholic Church, and received its name from the Babylonian goddess, *Ishtar*. Ishtar is the pagan god of fertility, love, and sex; and that is why eggs are a part of the modern Easter celebration. The same thing is true as to why rabbits are part of the pageantry. Although children use rabbits, colored eggs and green grass to celebrate Easter; adult Christians observe Easter as the day of our Lord's resurrection from the dead. Instead of calling this celebration *Easter*, we should call it *Firstfruits*. There are exactly 50 days (7 full Jewish weeks) and it always begins and ends on a Sunday, since it lasts exactly Seven weeks (49 days) and one day. The 50th and final day is called *Shavuot* by the Jews. In 1490 BC the Children of Israel left Egypt during the night of Nisan 15; Thursday on the Jewish calendar). Six days later they crossed the *Red Sea*. They emerged on the other side a free nation, miraculously saved from the armies of the Pharaoh when God drowned all of the pursuers after all of the Israelites had safely crossed. 50 days later, they reached Mt. Sinai in Arabia (Galatians 4:25). Moses immediately ascended the Mountain to speak to God, and three days later …. on the 53th day *after leaving Egypt*, Moses descended from the mountain with the 10-commandments (For more details see Phillips: The Book of Exodus; *Historical and Prophetic Truths*).

> ***Authors Comment***: It is well known that Moses assembled the Children of Israel and left the Land of Goshen on Nisan 15. The Jewish historian Josephus who lived at the time of Christ, wrote: The *Antiquity of the Jews*, The *Jewish Wars*, and *Against Apion*. In the Antiquity of the Jews, Josephus interprets the 430 years of Exodus 12:40 as starting with Abraham's entrance into Canaan and ending at the Exodus. Josephus states:
>
>> They left Egypt in the month Xanthicus (Ancient month of Nisan), on the fifteenth day of the lunar month; four hundred and thirty years after our forefather Abraham came into Canaan, but two hundred and fifteen years only after Jacob removed into Egypt Antiquities of the Jews, Chapter 15.2

What day of the week did Nisan 15 fall when the Exodus began? We can prove that Nisan 15 was a Thursday when the Exodus began. The following diagram shows the 1st 29 days of the 53-day Exodus.

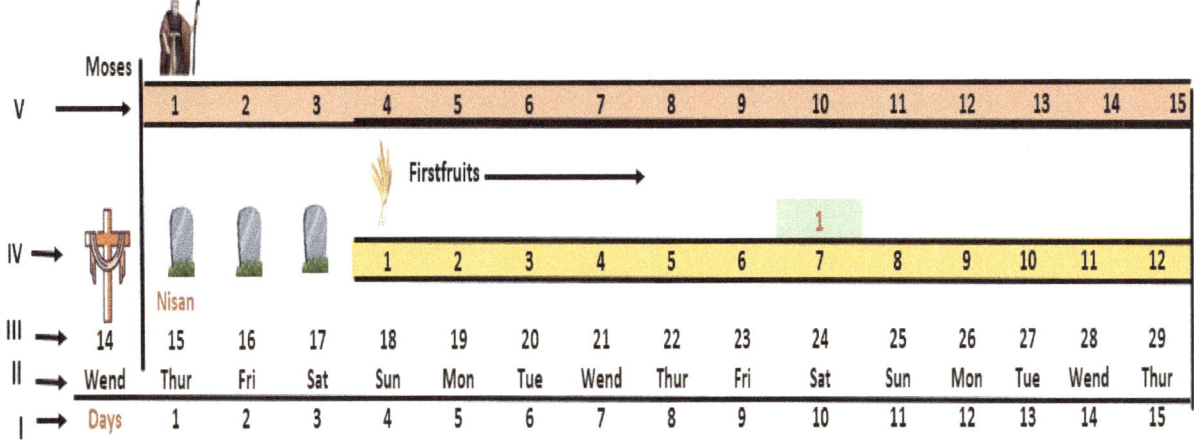

I. This is the Day of the Week (**M-F**)
II. This is the Number of Days (**Days**) elapsed from Nisan 15 (inclusive counting)
III. This is the Jewish Calendar Day (**Number**) starting on Nisan 14
IV. This is a Sequential Count of Days (**1,2…**) from the Feast of Firstfruits (Nisan 18) to the Feast of Shavuot (Pentecost) as specified in the Holy scriptures
V. This is a sequential count of days (**1,2…**) from when Moses left Egypt to when the Law was given at Mt Sinai

A Complete set of graphics is shown below

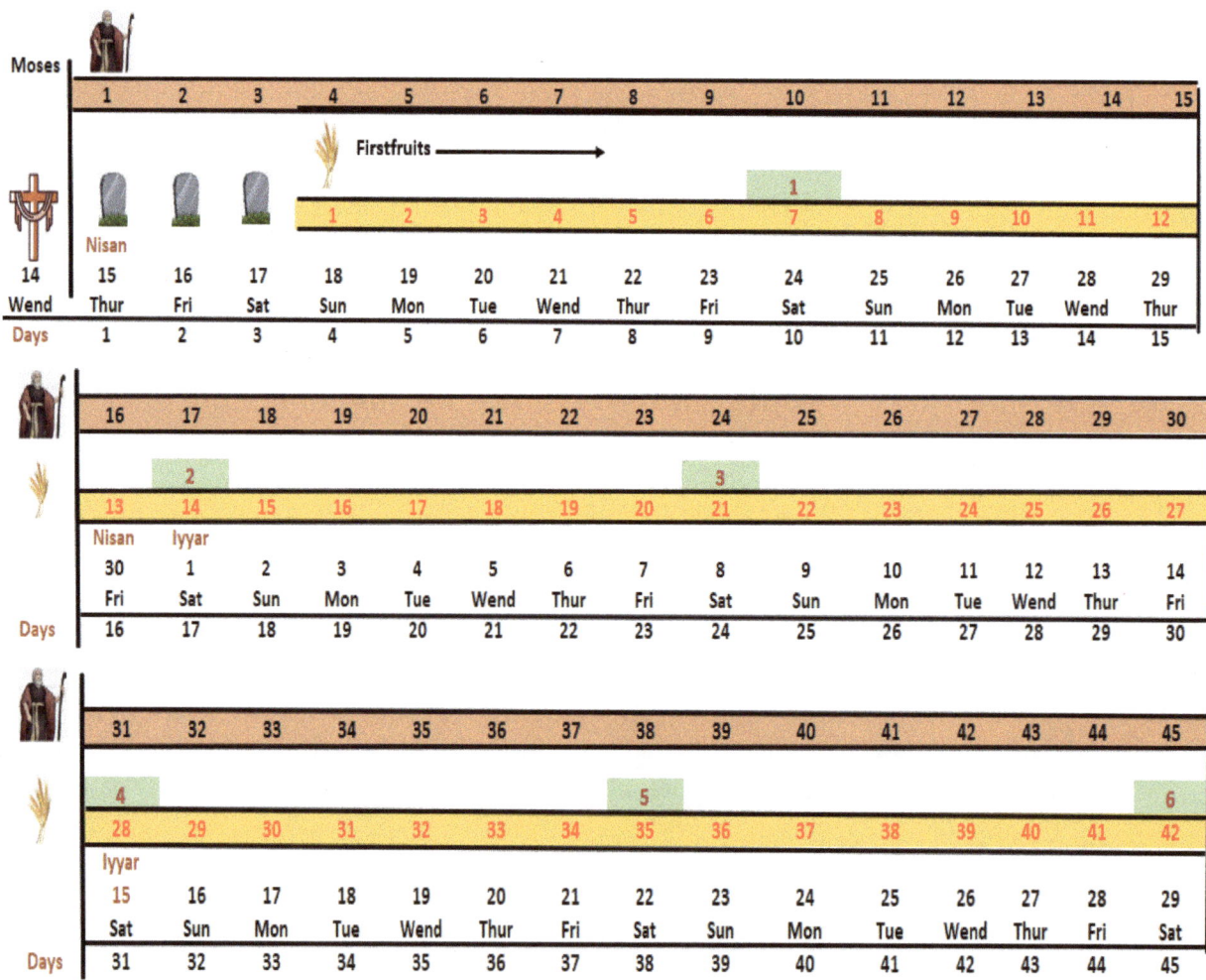

	46	47	48	49	50	51	52	53
							7	
	43	44	45	46	47	48	49	50
Sivan	1	2	3	4	5	6	7	8
	Sun	Mon	Tue	Wend	Thur	Fri	Sat	Sun
Days	46	47	48	49	50	51	52	53

These set of Tables graphically portray two different scenarios. The 1st is the Exodus journey of Moses from when he led the people out of Egypt until God gave them the Law at Mt. Sinai. The 2nd is the count from when Jesus Christ was crucified until the Holy Spirit fell on the Feast of Pentecost. The Exodus journey of Moses is shown in a *pink* timeline. The count to Pentecost is shown by a *gold* timeline. First, trace the 53-day trip of Moses from when he left Egypt until the law was received from God at Mt. Sinai. There is no doubt that Moses began the Exodus from Egypt on Nisan 15 (Exodus 12: 1-6, Exodus 12:29, Numbers 33:3), This is proof that Nisan 15 was a Thursday (trace counting diagrams). There is an ongoing debate as to when the Children of Israel actually left their houses. *Was it shortly after midnight or early the morning of Nisan 15?* The issue is debatable, but there is scriptural evidence that each family left their house early on the morning of Nisan 15 (Exodus 12: 10-22), Numbers 9:12). Either way, Moses led the people out of Egypt on Nisan 15, and that Christ was crucified on a Wednesday.

*And they took their journey from Elim, and all the congregation of the children of Israel came to the wilderness of Sin, which is between Elim and Sinai, on the **fifteenth day of the second month** after their departing out of the land of Egypt*   Exodus 16:1

From the above Tables, this is Iyyar 15.

In Exodus 19 we are told that Moses reached Mt. Sinai: *In the third month, when the children of Israel were gone forth out of the land of Egypt, **the same day** came they into the wilderness of Sinai* (Exodus 19:1) and camped before the mountain (Exodus 19:2). What does the phrase *same day* mean? It cannot mean on Nisan 15 so it must mean on the same day of the week. At this point, we must remember what day of the week that Jesus Christ was placed in the grave. There were three possibilities.

(1) Christ was placed in the grave on Wednesday, Nisan 14 before 6:00 PM.

Christ was in the grave Thursday night, Thursday day; Friday night, Friday day; Saturday night, Saturday day…...and He arose from the grave Saturday at 6:00 PM……3 days and 3 nights (Matthew 12:40)

(2) Christ was placed in the grave on Thursday, Nisan 14 before 6:00 PM

Christ was in the grave Friday night, Friday day; Saturday night, Saturday day; Sunday night…...and He arose from the grave Sunday at 6:00 AM……3 days and 3 nights………2 days and 3 nights.

(3) Christ was placed in the grave on Friday, Nisan 14 before 6:00 PM

Christ was in the grave Saturday night, Saturday day; Sunday night; and He arose from the grave Sunday at 6:00 AM......1 day and 2 nights.

The only scenario that does not violate the very words of Jesus Christ Himself is that the crucifixion was on Wednesday, Nisan 14. The following table shows what day of the week and the corresponding Gregorian Calendar Date Nisan 14 fell on in 28 AD - 34 AD. Almost all biblical theologians believe that Jesus died between 28 AD and 34 AD (Calculated by the *Abdicate Calendar Convertor*. Verified by the *Hebcal Calendar Convertor*).

Nisan 14 in the Years 28 AD - 34 AD

Year	Day	Date
28 AD	Monday	March 27
29 AD	Saturday	April 14
30 AD	Wednesday	April 3
31 AD	Monday	March 24
32 AD	Monday	April 12
33 AD	Friday	April 1
34 AD	Monday	March 20

Authors Comment: There are four popular choices for the year that Christ was crucified: 30 AD (Phillips and others), 32 AD (Sir Robert Anderson and others) and 33 AD (Roman Catholics and Roman Catholic Church). Parker and Dubberstein suggest that in 31 AD an extra month was added prior to Nisan 1. They suggest this was necessary because the crops were slow in maturing that year. The insertion of an extra month after the 6th month of Elul results in Nisan 14 being a Wednesday in 31 AD. This appears to be an assumption required to force a Wednesday for the Crucifixion in 31 AD. Does it matter? Not much….The key conclusion is that a Wednesday crucifixion is required to allign that day with scripture. For confirmation that 30 AD is the correct year: (See Phillips, The Birth and Death of Jesus Christ or Phillips, The Birth of Christ: *A Forinsic Analysis* and Coulter, The Day that Jesus the Christ Died . Without some sort of special calendar adjustment, there is but one Wednesday possibility according to the most reliable Calendar Convertors….30 AD.

The conclusion of this detailed analysis is that Jesus Christ died on Wednesday, Nisan 14 in 30 AD. By using the count to Pentecost from the Feast of Firstfruits as God specified, the Feast of Pentecost (Shavuot) will fall upon Sivan 8 every year (Not Sivan 6 as observed by modern Jews……See counting diagrams). This is the yellow line which places the Feast of Pentecost on a Sunday, Sivan 8……Exactly where it should be according to scripture.

Returning once again to the counting diagrams, note the passage of time (days) between when Moses left Egypt until he arrived at Mt. Sinai.

[1] ***In the third month*** (Sivan), *when the children of Israel were gone forth out of the land of Egypt,* ***the same day*** *(Thursday) came they into the wilderness of Sinai.*
[2] *For they were departed from Rephidim, and were come to the desert of Sinai, and had pitched in the wilderness;* ***and there Israel camped before the mount***   Exodus 19: 1-2

Examining the counting diagrams, Moses reached the base of Mt. Sinai after a 50-day journey. Note he arrived on Thursday, Sivan 5…... just as it is recorded in Exodus 19: 1-2. When Moses arrived on Sivan 5, he ascended the mountain to meet with God. God instructed him to descend Mt. Sinai and tell the people He would meet with them on the 3rd day.

*And be ready against the third day: for **the third day the LORD will come down** in the sight of all the people upon mount Sinai*
Exodus 19:11

[14] And Moses went down from the mount unto the people, and sanctified the people; and they washed their clothes.
[15] And he said unto the people, Be ready against the third day
Exodus 19: 14-15

Moses then ascended Mount Sinai once again with Aaron, and they talked to the Lord for 2-days.

And the LORD said unto him, Away, get thee down, and thou shalt come up, thou, and Aaron with you   Exodus 19:24

Three days after Moses arrived at Mt. Sinai, God spoke to all of the people and verbally spoke the 10 commandments (Exodus 20: 1-26). This is exactly as shown in the last counting diagram.

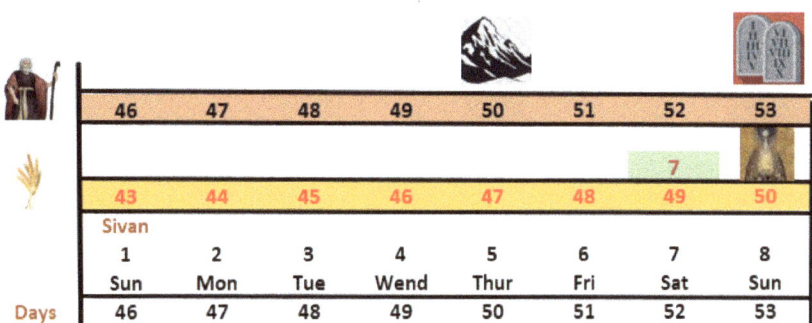

This detailed analysis yields several important results which will be new information to most students and scholars.

(1) The Exodus from Rameses to Mt. Sinai took 50 days
(2) The Law was given at Mt. Sinai on the 53rd day after Moses had left Rameses

41

(3) The popular assumption that the Law was given to Israel, and that the Holy Spirit fell upon the Jews in Jerusalem in 30 AD, were both on the same day (50th day) is correct; but it was on the 53rd day after Moses left Egypt and on the 50th day after the Feast of Firstfruits in 30 AD.

(4) The difference in the 53 days to the Giving of the Law to Moses and the people, and the Holy Spirit falling upon New Covenant Jews 50 days after the crucifixion, is that Moses started his 50 day journey to Mt. Sinai on Thursday, Nisan 15 and arrived at Mt. Sinai on Thursday, Sivan 5. The Law was given to Moses and the people 3-days later on Sunday, Sivan 8.

(5) After the Jordan River was crossed God instructed Israel:

[15] *And ye shall count unto you from the **morrow after the sabbath**, from the day that ye brought the sheaf of the wave offering; seven sabbaths shall be complete:*
[16] *Even **unto the morrow after the seventh sabbath** shall ye number fifty days; and ye shall offer a new meat offering unto the LORD*   Leviticus 23: 15-16

(6) Hence, the *Law* was given to Israel and the *Holy Spirit* both fell on the same day…. Sunday, Sivan 8.

> *Authors Comment:* Modern Jews *always* start the 50-day count to the *Feast of Shavuot* (Incorrectly) on *Nisan 16*. This 50-day count will end on *Sivan 6* (Incorrectly) every year. Modern Jews celebrate the Feast of Shavuot (Pentecost) on Sivan 6 ignoring God's instructions.

On the first day of the Feast of Firstfruits a remarkable thing happened. Just as Saturday, Nisan 17 was ending and Sunday, Nisan 18 was beginning, Jesus Christ rose from the Grave. Mary Magdelene and the apostles had no idea that this was pre-ordained since time began by God the Father (John 20: 8-9).

There are two things that Jesus Christ accomplished when He was crucified on Wednesday, Nisan 14 in 30 AD. (1) The 1st was to offer Himself as the perfect, sacrificial Lamb of God to once and for all settle the sin issue. Jesus said before He died: *all have sinned and fall short of the glory of God.* (Romans 3: 23-2). Since all have sinned, the only way to offer salvation to Jews and Gentiles alike was to eliminate forever the sin issue. All are now justified freely by his grace through the redemption that came by the sacrificial death of Jesus Christ. The gift of eternal life is now offered freely to all by *faith*. (2) Forgiveness of sin is not enough. When Christ rose from the dead, He guaranteed that anyone who believed upon His Holy Name would also follow Him from the grave. He was the *Firstfruits* of all who would become what we call a *born-again Christian* after His death and resurrection.

The resurrection is our blessed hope, and since it is so important to every Christian, it should be clear what took place when Christ ascended from the grave. Matthew, Mark, Luke and John all contain written records of what happened (Matthew 28: 1-10, Mark 16: 1-12, Luke 24: 1-12 and John 20: 1-18). Unfortunately, the four gospel accounts cannot be easily reconciled. After studying the 4 Gospels and asking the Holy spirit for help, the following scenario seem to reconcile and harmonize all 4 gospel accounts.

The Women Visit the Tomb

In the Gospel of Matthew (Matthew 28:9) we read that Mary Magdalene and Mary the mother of James encountered Jesus and they immediately took hold of His feet and worshipped Him. In the Gospel of John (John 20:17), we read that Mary Magdelene encountered Jesus outside the empty tomb, and she was warned by Christ: *touch me not.*

In the Gospel of Mark (Mark 16:1) and in Luke (Luke 24:1), Mary Magdelene, Mary mother of James and Solome *came to the tomb bringing spices* to finish anointing Jesus for burial with *certain others*. Matthew and John never mentioned anyone bringing spices. It is proposed that these and other difficulties can be resolved by recognizing that the these were not the same events at the same time, and that Mary Magdelene actually visited the tomb 3 times. The most likely scenario which resolves all conflicts is as follows.

1. Christ was placed on the Cross of Calvary at 9:00 AM (John 19:34); He was declared dead at 3:00 PM (Mark 15:35). To make sure He was dead, a Roman soldier pierced His side with a sword, and water and blood gushed forth (John 19: 34-35). As John testifies: *These things happened so that the scripture would be fulfilled: A bone of Him shall not be broken* (John 19:36, Exodus 12:36). This is also echoed prophetically in Psalm 34:20: *He* (God the Father) *protects all his bones, not one of them will be broken*. To the last detail of his death, Jesus fulfilled the prophecies concerning the Messiah, verifying that he was, as John the Baptist claimed: *the sacrificial Lamb of God* (John 1: 34-36). His pierced body is hastily removed from the cross after he died at 3:00 PM on Wednesday, Nisan 14. Several things rapidly took place at this time. Joseph of Arimathea had to visit with Herod and gain permission to bury Christ; Herod insisted that a Roman Centurion would testify that Christ was dead (Mark 15: 44-45); Joseph and several women moved the body of Christ into the tomb, and hastily covered it with fine linen and a napkin (Matthew 27:60); and the tomb was sealed with a large stone (Matthew 27:60). Mary Magdelene and Mary the mother of James were there (Mark 15:47). This had to all be completed by 6:00 PM when the High Holy Sabbath of Nisan 17 started. All of this suggests that there was not enough time to fully anoint and prepare Christ for burial.

2. In 30 AD, the crucifixion was on Wednesday, Nisan 14. Nisan 15 was a *high Sabbath day*, Nisan 16 (Friday) was a preparation day for the Sabbath day of Saturday, Nisan 17. The women rested according to the law.
3. A group of women including Mary M., Mary and Salome (Luke 23:55) agreed that they would return to finish the preparation of Christ for burial (Mark 16:1, Luke 24:1). A question which lingers is: *Where were the herbs and spices (80-100 Lbs.) bought and when were they prepared (Luke 23:56)?* They must have been bought and prepared on Friday, Nisan 16. The only other time would be after 6:00 PM on Nisan 17. The latter is possible but not likely. Where would they buy the ingredients and how would they prepare them in the dark?
4. It is well known that Mary Magdelene loved Christ greatly and became His disciple after Jesus cast out seven demons from Mary, restoring her sanity and redeeming her mental state (Luke 8:2). She was at the Crucifixion, and because of her love and devotion to Christ she wanted to revisit the tomb of Christ as soon as possible. This could be no earlier than the night of Sunday, Nisan 18 (Matthew 27: 62-66).
5. Mary Magdelene left for the tomb by herself sometime after 6:00 PM on Sunday, Nisan 18 while it was dark (John 20:1). There is no mention of anyone else who was with her or that she brought any herbs and spices. When she reached there, she discovered that the rock that sealed the tomb had been rolled away. In horror and panic, she did not even look inside but immediately turned and ran to the house of Peter (John 20:2) and said to them that the body of Christ had been stolen. John is staying with Peter, and they both immediately ran to the tomb (John 20:3). Both Peter and John ran ahead of Mary Magdelene who was obviously tired. John arrived first (John 20:4), and did not go in but stooped and saw the linen clothes folded neatly in a pile (John 20:5). Peter arrives and boldly

bolts into the tomb (John 20:6). He sees the linen clothes and also the napkin which covered His head (John 20:7). John now enters the tomb and *believed* (John 20:8). Believed what?.......Believed that the body of Christ had been stolen because: *For as yet they knew not the scripture, that he must rise again from the dead* (John 20:9). Believing that the body of Jesus had been stolen, both Peter and John leave the tomb and return to the house of Peter (John 20:10). Mary finally arrives, and without seeing either Peter or John she stands outside the tomb *weeping.* As she stands crying, she looks into the tomb for the first time (John 20:11). She sees two angels where Christ had laid, and they ask her: *Why are you crying?* She answers*: because the body of Christ has been stolen (*John 20: 12-13). As she turns away, she sees a man who she thinks is the gardener (caretaker). The man also asks *Why are you crying?* and then asks: *Who are you looking for?* (John 20: 14-16). Mary now fully turns to face the man, but she still did not recognize him (John 20:15). The man is the resurrected Jesus, and in love and compassion says: MARY. Oh, what joy! When we will also see Christ face to face, He will call us by name and we will also know Him.

6. Mary now knows that this is Jesus and cries: *Rabboni*…which means *teacher* in Hebrew. Before Mary can hold her precious Jesus, He tells her:

> *Touch me not; for I am not yet ascended to my Father: but go to my* **brethren***, and say unto them, I ascend unto my Father, and your Father; and to my God, and your God*
> John 20:17

Mary obeys, and runs to tell His *brethren*: *I have seen the risen Lord.* We now conjecture that Mary Magdelene meets with Mary the mother of James. She wants to see the empty tomb herself (Matthew 28:1). Matthew inserts a fact in Matthew 28:23.

7. When Mary M. arrived at the tomb earlier, the stone had been rolled away. It was moved by an angel of the Lord…. Not to let Jesus out but so that all who would come later could see He was not there.

8. When the two Mary's arrive, the same angel announces: *I Know why you are here, but Jesus has risen just as He said He would* (Mattthew 28: 5-6). *Now go, and tell the disciples of Jesus that He has risen, and that He will meet with them in Galilee* (Matthew 28:7). The two women depart immediately, but as they return to Jerusalem Christ suddenly meets them on the road and speaks: *All Hail……*and *they fell at His feet and held Him.* Halleluiah!!!! (Matthew 28: 8-10). Christ has just ascended to the Father and has been glorified. NOTE that this *proves* that Christ rose and ascended to the Father before dawn on Sunday, Nisan 18.

This squares the two Gospel records of John and Matthew, but what about Mark and Luke? Note that the records of John and Matthew contain no reference to anointing or spices. This is the key to resolving all apparent discrepancies between Matthew, Mark, Luke and John.

The four apostles document *two visits* to the tomb by both Mary Magdalen and Peter. Mark and Luke record what happened early Sunday morning.

Now upon the first day of the week, **very early in the morning**, *they came unto the sepulcher, bringing the spices which they had prepared, and* **certain others** *with them*   Luke 24:1

[1] *And when the sabbath was past, Mary Magdalene, and Mary the mother of James, and Salome, had bought sweet spices, that they might come and anoint him.*

[2] *And very early in the morning the first day of the week, they came unto the sepulcher* **at the rising of the sun**.
[3] *And they said among themselves:* **Who shall roll us away the stone from the door of the sepulcher?**   Mark 16: 1-3

1.0   The first difficulty is that Mary Magdelene and the other Mary are with Salome and *others* (Luke 24:1, Mark 16:1). Both Mary's knew that the tomb was empty and that Christ had risen (Matthew 28:1), so it is conjectured that they were not with the other women as they approached the tomb…… We are simply not told. Perhaps both had slept late after a busy night…. perhaps they mean to meet the others on time, but were just late.

2.0   In any case, Salome and the others were *not* aware that Christ had risen because they asked on the way: *Who will roll away the stone that sealed the door*? (Mark 16:3). When they finally arrived, they were surprised to find that the stone had already been moved away (Luke 24:2).

3.0   As they looked into the tomb, Christ was not there but they saw the same two angels that Mary had seen previously (Luke 24:4, John 20:12).

4.0   As they peered inside the tomb, the angels inquired: *Why do you seek the living among the dead? He whom you seek is not here. Don't you remember that he said He would rise from the grave after 3 days?* (Luke 24: 5-7). Then: *the women remembered His words* (Luke 24:8).

> ***Authors Comment:*** From Luke 24:8 we discover another interesting fact. The women remembered that Christ had told them that He would rise from the dead. The apostles did not remember what He said (Mark 16:11, Luke 24:12).
> The women returned from the tomb and told everyone that Christ had risen (Luke 24:10). In Luke 24:10 we are told that

the news was spread by the other women plus Mary Magdelene, the other Mary and a woman called Joanna. This is a hint that the two Mary's were not recruited to spread the news until later, or they could have met the other women as they returned and believed their report …...We are not told these details.

5.0 One thing is certain, as the women spread the news that Christ had risen……*no one believed their report* (Luke 24:11). But Peter evidently believed what they said and arose to probably hoping to talk to the angels himself (Luke 24:12). When he arrived at the tomb, it was empty except for the linen clothes. He evidently still did not believe that Christ had risen (Luke 24:12).

> ***Authors Comment***: Peter was obviously confused and was not thinking clearly. If he had remembered the words of Christ that He would rise after 3 days, or if he had questioned the status of the linens…he would know that the body of Christ had not been stolen. Anyone who would steal the body of Christ would not have taken the time to remove His linens and fold them neatly into two separate piles. The disciples of Christ had been told to meet Jesus Christ on a mountain in Galilee. The 11 disciples, including Peter, had been told to meet Jesus Christ in the upper room in Jerusalem. All male Jews were also going to be at the Feast of Pentecost.

After searching for a way to resolve all inconsistencies in the Gospel accounts of Matthew, Mark, Luke and John these are my conclusions. There were three separate trips to the tomb: two just after 6:00 PM on Saturday while it was dark, and one by the women with spices and anointing oil. I could be wrong, please let me know if you disagree. In reality, it is not important except to once again show that the scriptures are inerrant in content. The important thing is that Jesus Christ was crucified, dead, and buried and after 3 days and 3 nights He arose from the grave at 6:00 PM on Nisan 17 one second before the night of Nisan 18. Christ ascended to God and was the *Firstfruits* of all who would follow his resurrection and be glorified at the *Rapture.*

Christ arose just as Sunday was *dawning* or about to start just after 6:00 PM Saturday. There is no proof in the scriptures that Christ rose from the grave just before 6:00 AM on Sunday morning. This is another story that the Catholic Church instituted. To be clear, there is no problem in celebrating Christ's resurrection at a *sunrise service* on Sunday morning, it is holy that we should do so. The point is that Christ rose early that previous evening just as Sunday, Nisan 18 began and not at sunrise. (For a further discussion and confirmation of this truth, see Coulter: *The Day Jesus the Christ Died.*

But now is Christ risen from the dead, and become the Firstfruits of them that slept   I Corinthians 15:20

Christ was the *First of the Firstfruits*. He was not the only person that had been resurrected from the dead; but he was the first to ascend to heaven, receive His glorified body, and not taste death again.

For if the Firstfruits be holy, the lump is also holy: and if the root be holy, so are the branches   Romans 11:16

Christ is the vine and we are the branches. Christ spoke of this during his earthly ministry.

I am the vine, ye are the branches: He that abides in me, and I in him, the same bringeth forth much fruit: for without me ye can do nothing John 15:5

Jesus also spoke of the truth that one must die to Christ to yield the precious fruit.

And Jesus answered them, saying: The hour is come, that the Son of man should be glorified. Verily, verily, I say unto you, except a corn of wheat Fall into the ground and die, it abides alone: but if it dies, it bringeth forth much fruit. He that loveth his life shall lose it; and he that hates his life in this world shall keep it unto life eternal. If any man serves me, let him follow me; and where I am, there shall also my servant be: if any man serves me, him will my Father honor John 12: 23-26

The Apostle Paul made an astonishing statement in his first letter to Corinth.

But now is Christ risen from the dead, and become the Firstfruits of them that slept. For since by man came death, by man came also the resurrection of the dead. For as in Adam all die, even so in Christ shall all be made alive. But every man in his own order: Christ the Firstfruits; afterward they that are Christ's at his coming. Then cometh the end, when he shall have delivered up the kingdom to God, even the Father; when he shall have put down all rule and all authority and power
I Corinthians 15:20-24

Christ is clearly called the *Firstfruits* of all that *slept* (died). Paul then goes on to say that one day there will be a resurrection of the dead and a Rapture of all living Saints. Shortly after that, the end (of the Church Age) will come to an end and all *powers, authorities and rulers* will be put under His feet (Ephesians 1: 22-23).

The Feast of Shavuot (Pentecost)

The *Feast of Shavuot* is called the *Feast of Weeks* (Exodus 34:22 Deuteronomy 16:10, II Chronicles 8:13) because it is the 50th day after a count of 7 weeks starting on the Spring *Feast of Firstfruits*. Properly determined, it will always fall on a Sunday. The Firstfruits for the *wheat* crop is dedicated on that day (Numbers 28:26). Christians and modern-day Jews refer to this day as *Pentecost*. This is one of the three holy Feasts (Passover, Pentecost and Tabernacles) that God requires all males to attend.

In the 1st Century AD, there was some controversy involved in when the Feast of Pentecost should be observed. The problem arose because there are *two* sabbath days that were observed during the Feast of Unleavened Bread: (1) The weekly High Holy Day on the 1st day of the Feast of Unleavened Bread and the only Saturday that fell during the Feast of Unleavened Bread (2) The Sunday following the only Jewish Sabbath (Saturday) which fell during the 7-day Feast of Unleavened Bread. The High Holy day of Nisan 15 was the interpretation of the *Sadducees,* and the Sunday which followed the Jewish Sabbath day of Saturday was chosen by the *Pharisees*. This is important, because the 50-day count to the Feast of Shavuot (Day of Pentecost) began on the 1st day following the correct Sabbath. The controversy can be settled by the following commands of God.

[15] *And ye shall count unto you from the morrow after the sabbath, from the day that ye brought the sheaf of the wave offering; seven sabbaths shall be complete*

[16] *Even unto the morrow after the seventh sabbath shall ye number fifty days*   Leviticus 23: 15-16

Note that there are no exceptions to the commands of God. What He demands must be followed to the letter. Since there can be no exceptions to the rule, the correct interpretation of when to start the 50-day count to Shavuot (Pentecost) must be valid for the Feasts which occurred in 30 AD. The following graphic illustrates the days and dates of the 4 Spring Feasts in 30 AD.

There are three important instructions in Leviticus 23: 15-16 which support the 1st century Pharisees: (1) The 50-day count to Shavuot must begin on the 1st day (Sunday) which follows the weekly Sabbath day of Nisan 17. This Sunday is clearly identified as the day that the Firstfruit Offering is to be waved before the Lord (Leviticus 23:16). 7 Sabbaths must be included in the 50-day count. The context of Leviticus 23:15 demands that these 7 sabbath days be Jewish Sabbath days (Saturday). The following figure shows the Spring Jewish calendar in 30 AD.

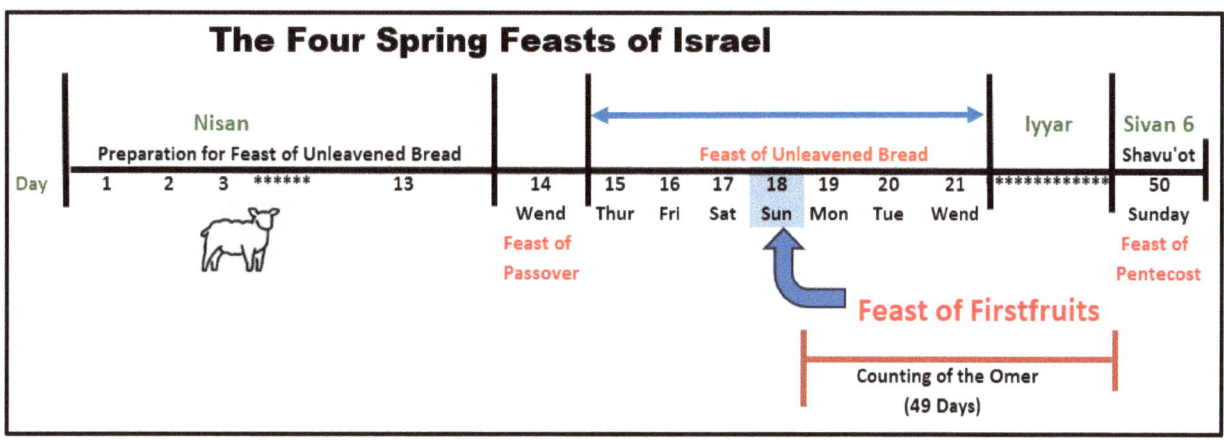

The following graphic illustrates the Spring months of Nisan, Iyyar and Sivan in 30 AD.

Nisan 14 in 30 AD was Wednesday, April 5

Case I: 50-Day count to Feast of Pentecost begins on Nisan 16

Starting on the day after the High Holy day of Nisan 15 (A Sabbath day which is Friday, Nisan 16) and counting 49 days, we arrive at Sivan 6.

This would place the *Feast of Pentecost* on *Sivan 7 every year*. Note that Sivan 7 is on a Saturday. But the Lord commanded that the Feast of Pentecost be observed on a Sunday. …. Clearly something is wrong.

Case II: 50-Day count begins on day after the Feast of Firstfruits

Notice once again what the Lord said in Leviticus: *And ye shall count unto you from the **morrow after the sabbath**, from the **day that ye brought the sheaf of the wave offering**; **seven sabbaths shall be complete**: Even **unto the morrow after the seventh sabbath shall ye number fifty days**.*

From the above calendar of the Spring months in 30 AD, the 50-day count to Pentecost would begin on Sunday, Nisan 18. The 1st 7-days end on Saturday, Nisan 24. The 2nd week would start on Nisan 25 and end on Saturday, Iyyar 1. Continuing a count of 49 days, 7 weeks of 7 days. …. the 49th day is on Saturday, Sivan 7. The 50th day is on Sunday, Nisan 8. This is exactly what the Lord commanded. The 50-day count to Pentecost will always *begin* on the day of the Feast of Firstfruits (Sunday), and The Feast of Pentecost will *always* be on a Sunday, but the Hebrew calendar date and the Gregorian calendar date of Pentecost will usually change from year to year. It is clear that the Pharisees were correct.

The first 49 days of the 50-day count between the Feast of Firstfruits and the Day of Pentecost is called the *Counting of the Omer* by the Jews. An Omer is about two quarts. The **Torah** (Incorrectly) dictates the Counting of the Omer as follows.

> "You shall count from the eve of the second day of Pesach, when an Omer of grain is to be brought as an offering, seven complete weeks. The day after the seventh week of your counting will make fifty days, and you shall present a new meal offering to God"

Jews today hold the Feast of Pentecost on the wrong day. They have fixed the day of Pentecost on Sunday, Sivan 6 This dictates that the Jews *always* start the count to Pentecost on the *2cd day of the Feast of Unleavened Bread,* (Nisan 16) This is clearly wrong, but it shows that the Jews adopted the counting scheme of the Sadducees in the 1st Century AD and it continues (incorrectly) until today. Karaite Jews and Israelite Samaritans begin counting the *Omer* (correctly) on the day after the weekly Sabbath during Passover, rather than on the second day of the Feast of Unleavened Bread. (the 16th of Nisan).

Jews observe the *Feast of Shavuot* (Feast of Pentecost) to celebrate the giving of the Torah on Mount Sinai. It's taken from Leviticus 23 and Numbers 28. On the Feast of Shavuot, two loaves of wheat are prepared with leaven and offered to the Lord. This is an offering of thanks to God for Israel's bountiful harvest. On the morning of the first day of Shavuot, many gather in the synagogue to read Exodus 19 and 20, which describes the giving of the Law at Mount Sinai. All stand when the Ten Commandments are read, honoring this important day in Jewish history. Jewish tradition teaches that on the day of Pentecost the law was given to Israel on Mt. Sinai. There were 53 days that elapsed between when the Children of Israel left Egypt and the law was given at Mt. Sinai. The word *Pentecost* is derived from the Greek word *Penta*, which means *fifty*. Israel departed Egypt on Thursday, Nisan 15 and *arrived* at Mt. Sinai 50 days later. When Moses reached Mt. Sinai, God told him to speak to the people and purify themselves for two days. On the 3rd day, God would descend from Mt. Sinai and speak to the people.

There is a legend taught by the Rabbis that when God told Abraham to sacrifice his son Issac as a burnt offering. Abraham did as he was told. He ascended Mt. Moriah and prepared His son for sacrifice (Genesis 22: 1-19). He bound Isaac and placed him upon an altar of sacrifice. Just as Abraham was about to kill his son, God stayed his hand and told him to look upon a nearby bush. Abraham saw a ram that had been caught up in the bush and he sacrificed the ram instead of his son. The ram was completely consumed as a burnt offering except for the two horns. It is taught that one horn would be blown at Mt. Sinai when God gave the law to the people, and the other (the last horn) would be blown on some future Feast of Trumpets when God will resurrect all dead Jews and call all (alive or dead) to Him. (Does this sound familiar to Christians?)

When God descended Mt. Sinai to give the 10-Commandments, a shofar (rams horn) was blown; louder, louder and louder fire fell from the sky and the ground shook (Exodus 18:15). As Israel stood trembling in fear, the Torah and the 10-commandments were given. It is taught that as God spoke, His words were heard by all people in every nation of the world in 70 foreign languages. The Jewish Midrash teaches that as God spoke, the words went forth as a fiery cloud of fire. This cloud descended upon all who were gathered at Mt. Sinai and another voice asked: *Do you accept this command of God?* And the people answered: *Yes*.

Shavuot (Pentecost) is the final (4th) Festival of the Spring. By the 1st century AD, the entire set of Feasts: Passover, Unleavened Bread, Firstfruits and Shavuot became known as the *Passover Season*. The *Feast of Firstfruits* in the Spring is celebrated as the beginning of the Barley harvest, and The *Feast of Shavuot in the Fall* is the beginning of the wheat harvest.

This concludes our study of the Feast of Pentecost as observed by the orthodox Jews. It clearly shows that the Torah and Rabbis who teach that the Torah is inerrant, and often violate the Biblical commands of God. This is not surprising since the first 4 Spring Feasts of Israel also teach and prophesy of the 1st coming of our Lord Jesus Christ.

Messianic Application
Shavuot is an important Feast to all Christians, although it is not generally understood because most Christians do not study the 7 Feasts of Israel. The Jews received the Law at

Mt. Sinai on this day during the Exodus in 1450 BC, and Christians received the promise of the Holy spirit on this day in 30 AD. When Jesus Christ died on the cross of Calvary; the Levitical Priesthood, daily Temple sacrifices and the Law were all finished. Jesus Christ is now our eternal High Priest who gave Himself as the perfect sacrificial lamb of God. The weight of the Law was lifted, and the tablets of stone on which the 10-commandments were written were replaced by laws which is written on the heart.

*For this is the covenant that I will make with the house of Israel after those days, saith the Lord; I will put my laws into their mind, and write them in their **heart**s: and I will be to them a God, and they shall be to me a people*   Hebrews 8:10

Salvation under the New Covenant is by *faith*.

When Jesus Christ spoke to the women after His crucifixion, he commanded them to go and tell all of his disciples and His apostles to go to Jerusalem and wait for the promise of the Holy Spirit.

[2] Until the day in which he was taken up, after that he through the Holy Ghost had given commandments unto the apostles whom he had chosen:
[3] To whom also he shewed himself alive after his passion by many infallible proofs, being seen of them forty days, and speaking of the things pertaining to the kingdom of God:
[4] And, being assembled together with them, commanded them that they should not depart from Jerusalem, but wait for the promise of the Father, which, saith he, ye have heard of me   Acts 1: 2-4

Fifty-three (53) days after the crucifixion of Jesus Christ these words were fulfilled. This is exactly the same number of days from when Moses left Egypt until the Law was given to the people at Mt Sinai.

> *Authors Comment:* it is not uncommon to read that the 10 Commandments were given by God at Mt. Sinai 50 days after Moses left Egypt, but this is incorrect. To satisfy type and antitype, giving of the law at Mt. Sinai in the Old Testament must correspond to what happened on the Feast of Pentecost in Jerusalem in the New Testament. The children of Israel followed Moses for 50 days until they reached Mt. Sinai. Moses ascended Mt. Sinai and God told the people by Moses to consecrate themselves until the 3rd day, and God would descend the mountain and speak. The Law was given 53 days after they left Egypt. In 30 AD, Jesus Christ died on the Cross of Calvary on Wednesday, Nisan 14 and then rose from the grave 3 days and 3 nights later as Saturday, Nisan 17 came to an end at 6:00 PM. On Nisan 18 (Sunday), Christ ascended to His father and became the Firstfruits offering. The 50-day count to Pentecost began on Sunday, Nisan 18 and ended 50-days later on Sunday Sivan 8. *Both* the Feast of Pentecost (New Testament) and the Feast of Shavuot (Old Testament) began on a Thursday and ended on a Sunday. The type and antitype are satisfied exactly as they must. Note that this proves that Christ was crucified on a Wednesday, Nisan 14. This does not prove that the crucifixion was in 30 AD. However, 30 AD is shown to be the correct year by Phillips, The Birth of Christ: *A Forensic Analysis* and by Coulter, *The Day Jesus the Christ Died*.

The day that the Exodus from Egypt began was Thursday, Nisan 15 and it was exactly the same as the 1st day that Jesus Christ lay in the grave. Jesus rose from the grave 3 days later. In typology, a Friday crucifixion declared by the Roman Catholic Church and the subsequent resurrection from the grave on Sunday is impossible. The Israelites took 47 days until they reached Mt. Sinai on the Arabian Peninsula. The apostle Paul clearly said that Mt. Sinai was in the Arabian Peninsula (Galatians 4: 22-26. It is located in the Land of Midian where Moses spent 40 years tending sheep for his *father-in-law* Jethro, the priest of Midian (Exodus

3:1). The Lord told the people to sanctify themselves for two days (Gen 19:10), and on the *third* day He would come down to them in a cloud. On the 53rd *day* after leaving Tel el-Dab'a (ancient Rameses), in the northeast Nile Delta the Lord kept his promise and appeared to the people. A *Shofar* (trumpet made of a ram's horn) was loudly sounded: louder, and louder, and louder until *fire* was seen on the mountain. A mighty wind blew and the ground shook as if an earthquake was going to occur. At that point God began to deliver the law to Moses and the nation of Israel. It is taught that every nation and every tongue heard the Lord in their own language. According to tradition, there was the Hebrew language and 69 other languages spoken throughout the world. In a miraculous and divine act, the voice of God was divided into *70 different tongues*. It is also taught by the Rabbis that as God spoke, the Children of Israel not only heard the words but actually saw each word emerging from the cloud as *tongues of fire*. The words encircled the camp and then entered each person individually. After each commandment was given, God asked: **Do you accept upon yourself this commandment?** and everyone present answered *yes*. The tongues of fire then fell upon stone tablets and the words of the law were recorded. (Joseph Good, *Rosh Hashanah and the Messianic Kingdom to Come*) The Jewish Feast of Shavuot commemorates these events on Sivan 6 every year, but the correct biblical day is on the Sivan 8.

The Holy Spirit in each born-again Christian compels each New Covenant Christian to live by the law… not the written law but within the spirit of the law. Paul is writing to both devout Jews and to new Jewish Christians in Rome about the role of the law in every Christians life. Some saw the forgiveness of sin by Jesus Christ as a license to commit sin.

[1] *What shall we say then? Shall we continue in sin, that grace may abound?*
[2] *God forbid. How shall we, that are dead to sin, live any longer therein?*

15] *What then? shall we sin, because we are not under the law, but under grace? God forbid.*   Romans 6:1-2,15

Paul said: *God forbid*. He further explained that an election of Jews would inherit this promise in Jesus Christ.

[5] *Even so then at this present time also there is a remnant according to the election of grace.*
[6] *And if by grace, then is it no more of works: Otherwise, grace is no more grace. But if it be of works, then is it no more grace: Otherwise, work is no more work.*   Romans 7: 5-6

Every person is born under the curse of Adam with a sin-nature, but a person born under the New Covenant is not condemned under the law, but is held to a higher standard by the laws which are written in their heart. God spoke of this New Covenant through the prophet Jeremiah.

[31] *Behold, the days come, saith the LORD, that I will make a new covenant with the house of Israel, and with the house of Judah:*
[32] *Not according to the covenant that I made with their fathers in the day that I took them by the hand to bring them out of the land of Egypt; which my covenant they brake, although I was an husband unto them, saith the LORD:*
[33] *But this shall be the covenant that I will make with the house of Israel; After those days, saith the LORD, I will put my law in their inward parts, and write it in their hearts; and will be their God, and they shall be my people.*   Jeremiah 31: 31-33

Paul confirmed this in his letter to the Romans.

[12] *Wherefore the law is holy, and the commandment holy, and just, and good.*
[13] *Was then that which is good made death unto me? God forbid. But sin, that it might appear sin, working death in me by that which is good; that sin by the commandment might become exceeding sinful.*

[14] *For we know that the law is spiritual: but I am carnal, sold under sin.*   Romans 7: 12-14

The Day of Pentecost (Acts 2) in the year that Christ died was a day when believers were circumcised in the heart inwardly and were then able to express their spiritual gifts outwardly. This time when the Holy Spirit would come was prophesied in Joel 2:28. Jesus used this Jewish Feast to show that even though He was gone, He could still work in our lives by fulfilling His promise to send what His (our) Father had promised (Luke 24:29).

As another sign that these two holidays are connected, we can look at some of their end results. On the day the law was given, Israel was in a great state of sin because they had worshipped the golden calf while Moses was on Mt. Sinai talking to God. As a result, God acting through Moses ordered the killing of those who insisted on remaining faithful to idols. Around 3000 people were killed that day (Exodus 32: 26-28). On Pentecost, the day that the Holy Spirit came, type was again fulfilled in antitype when 3000 people were saved on the day of Pentecost (Acts 2:41).

In the first case (the giving of the law), Israel was brought together *by the law*; in the latter, believers in Christ were bonded together *by the Holy Spirit*. When Christ ascended from the grave, he commanded his disciples to *go unto Jerusalem* and wait for the promise of the Holy Spirit.

[1] *And when the day of Pentecost was fully come, they were all with one accord in one place.*
[2] *And suddenly there came a sound from heaven as of a rushing mighty wind, and it filled all the house where they were sitting.*
[3] *And there appeared unto them cloven tongues like as of fire, and it sat upon each of them.*
[4] *And they were all filled with the Holy Ghost, and began to speak with other tongues, as the Spirit gave them utterance.*
[5] *And there were dwelling at Jerusalem Jews, devout men, out of every*

nation under heaven.
[6] Now when this was noised abroad, the multitude came together, and were confounded, because that every man heard them speak in his own language.   Acts 2:1-6

What an amazing event!! On the very day of the week and on the same Jewish calendar day that God gave the law to the people on Mt. Sinai, Jesus Christ gave the Holy Spirit to his chosen people. The Falling of the Holy Spirit at Pentecost in 30 AD almost exactly paralleled the giving of the law 1500 years earlier. The *Old Covenant* was based upon man keeping the law, which was impossible. The law was written on tablets of stone. The *New Covenant* was based upon *faith*, and written on the heart of every man. The impossible task of living a perfect life under the law was fulfilled in every way by our Lord Jesus Christ, who then imputed His righteousness to all who believed in His name. Only Jesus Christ fulfilled every *jot and tidle* of the law (Matthew 5:18). He was our *perfect Passover sacrifice for sin*, the Lamb of God. He was the *Firstfruits* offering waved before the Lord by Christ himself. He was both the *offerer* and the *offering*, our eternal High Priest (Hebrews 5: 1-10).

The old covenant that God had established with His people required obedience to the Old Testament Mosaic law. Because the *wages of sin are death* (Romans 6:23), the law required that people perform rituals and sacrifices in order to please God and temporarily cover their sins. The prophet Jeremiah predicted that there would be a time when God would make a new covenant with the nation of Israel.

The day will come said the Lord, when I will make a new covenant with the people of Israel and Judah... But this is the new covenant I will make with the people of Israel on that day, says the Lord. I will put my law in their minds, and I will write them on their hearts. I will be their God, and they will be my people   Jeremiah 31:31, 33.

Jesus Christ came to fulfill all of the Law of Moses (Matthew 5:17) and create a New Covenant between God and His people. He is now our eternal High Priest who sits on the throne of God and continually intercedes for us.

This is the covenant that I will make with them after those days, saith the Lord, I will put my laws into their hearts, and in their minds will I write them   Hebrews 10:16

The Old Covenant was written in stone, but the New Covenant is written on our hearts, made possible only by faith in Christ who shed His own blood to atone for the sins of the world.

And he took bread, and gave thanks, and broke it, and gave unto them, saying: This is my body which is given for you: this do in remembrance of me. Likewise, also the cup after supper, saying, this cup is the New Testament in my blood, which is shed for you   Luke 22:19-20

Now that we are under the new covenant, we are not under the penalty of the law. All now given the opportunity to receive salvation as a free gift (Ephesians 2:8-9) by faith…. Jews and Gentiles alike. Through the life-giving Holy Spirit who lives in all believers (Romans 8:9-11), we can now share in the inheritance of Christ.

For this reason, Christ is the mediator of a new covenant, that those who are called may receive the promised eternal inheritance—now that He has died as a ransom to set them free from the sins committed under the first covenant   Hebrews 9:15

[3] *For what the law could not do, in that it was weak through the flesh, God sending his own Son in the likeness of sinful flesh, and for sin, condemned sin in the flesh:*
[4] *That the righteousness of the law might be fulfilled in us, who walk not after the flesh, but after the Spirit*   Romans 8:34

Summary of the First Four (Spring) Feasts of Israel
The Spring Feasts of Israel are (1) Passover, (2) Unleavened Bread, (3) Firstfruits and (4) Pentecost. Each of these Feasts was to provide historical and prophetic truth to the Children of Israel. Christ fulfilled each of these first four Feasts at the end of his 3.5-year earthly ministry. ***Passover***: Christ was the perfect Passover Lamb, slain from the foundation of the world. ***Unleavened Bread***: Christ was without sin (leaven). He fulfilled the laws given to Moses by God in every way. He is our *bread of life*, and whosoever will eat of His bread will never hunger. ***Firstfruits***: Christ was the perfect Firstfruits offering waved before the Lord and fully accepted. He was the *first* to be raised from the grave never to die again. ***Pentecost***: Christ ratified the *new covenant* on the Feast of Pentecost 50 days after he arose from the grave, He offered the Holy Spirit as our comforter and guarantee. Salvation is now offered free to all who believe that Jesus Christ is the only Son of God. The curse of the law has been replaced by amazing grace. We who are now called *Christians* can live life *more abundantly*. Every feast was a *moed*, a *set time* or an *appointed time*. The Feasts are also called a *holy convocation*. The Hebrew word for convocation means *rehearsal*. Paul referred to this:

Let no one judge you in food or in drink, or regarding a festival or a new moon or Sabbaths, which are a shadow of things to come, but the substance is of Christ   Colossians 2: 16-17

It is more than interesting that God commanded that every Jewish male appear in Jerusalem at the Feast of Unleavened Bread; the Feast of Pentecost; and the Feast of Tabernacles (Exodus 23:14, Deuteronomy 16:6). God was not only calling Israel to a time of remembrance, but he was preparing Israel for the appearance of their long-awaited Messiah in the person of Jesus Christ. All males were to witness the crucifixion of Christ (Passover) in 30 AD which was the day before the Feast of Unleavened Bread Started at 6:00 PM). The *Paracletes (*Holy Spirit) fell on the Feast of Shavuot (Pentecost); All Jewish males (and their families) who will accept Christ as their savior will be required to participate in the last Feast of Tabernacles to celebrate Christ's victory at Armageddon (Zach 14:16-19). It is strange that after all that was prophesied in the Old Testament, and all that was written by the prophets of His ministry here on earth, that the Children of Israel failed to recognize or accept Christ as their long-awaited Messiah. We have shown how Christ satisfied and fulfilled each of the four Spring festivals at exactly the appointed times; on exactly the appointed days; and exactly in type and substance.

Date	Feast or Event	Typology	Fulfillment
Nisan 10	The Passover Lamb is Selected. *"Bring an unblemished Lamb into the house on Nisan 10, Four days before it is to be slain And inspect it for spot or blemish"* Ex.12:3-6	God commands Israel in Egypt To select a Passover Lamb for slaughter On Nisan 14.	Jesus, the perfect Lamb of God, arrives in Bethany four days Before his crucifixion. He stood In the temple each day and was questioned by the Pharisees and Sadducees to find fault in him
Date	Feast or Event	Exodus Typology	Fulfillment by Christ
Nisan 15	First day of the Feast of Unleavened bread. A loaf of bread is baked from the Firstfruits of	The Pharaoh let *"the Children of Israel go"* after his firstborn son was slain.	Christ lay in the grave the first day. He is the *"loaf without leaven"*. He said *"I am the*

	Barley (Old Testament Saints). It was prepared without leaven. It was offered to the Lord "*with fire*".	The departure is in haste. The bread they took with them was unleavened	*bread of life*". He is the "*first*" and only to live a sinless life under the law. John said he will "*baptize you with water and fire*"
Nisan 15-21	The Feast of Unleavened Bread lasted 7 days. Both the first and last day of the feast were "*high holy*" days… Sabbath days	The Children of Israel ate unleavened bread until God gave them "*manna*" from heaven.	Christ said "I am the Bread of Life". He was the true bread without leaven. He was sinless and blameless.
First Sunday in the Feast of Unleavened Bread	Feast of Firstfruits starts on this day…always a Sunday. The Feast lasts 50 days. Every day a sheath of the emerging wheat crop is "*waved*" before the Lord. Also called the "Feast of Weeks".	On this day the Children of Israel crossed over the "*Sea of Reeds*", and was saved from death at the Pharaoh's hand. They emerged a new Nation under God.	Christ arose from the dead on this day. He was the "*Firstfruit*" unto God of all who will someday also rise from the grave by believing upon His name.
50 days from the Feast of Firstfruits	The Feast of Pentecost or Shavuot. "Penta" means fifty. Pentecost occurs 50 days	The Nation of Israel received the law from God at Mt. Sinai. The	On the Day of Pentecost Christ fulfilled his promise to leave with us

	after the first Sabbath (Saturday) in the Feast of Unleavened bread.	law was written on tablets of stone. The Levitical Priesthood was established. The High Priest was anointed to serve as the intercessor between man and God	an advocate: The Holy Spirit. On the day of Pentecost, the Holy Spirit fell on the disciples and 5,000 people were saved. The new covenant based upon grace replaced the old covenant based upon the law. The new law of grace is written in the heart and not in stone

The first four Feasts of Israel have been satisfied both spiritually and physically. Their implications to the Jewish Exodus from Egypt or to the 1st coming of Jesus Christ cannot be understood by either Jew or Gentile unless they are carefully studied.

On the Feast of Shavuot there were two loaves of bread that were baked with Wheat and both had leaven! How strange…....Leaven is a type of sin…. Why would God want to command such a thing? Here we see Christ once again in the Jewish Feasts. When Christ established the New Covenant on Calvary Hill, He did four unprecedented things: (1) He replaced the written Law on tablets of stone with unwritten laws that were written in the heart (2) He completely eradicated the sin issue and by His sacrificial death He forgave all sins of mankind…. Past, Present and Future (3) He broke down the barrier which existed between Jew and Gentile (4) He replaced the Old Covenant with a new and better New Covenant. Eternal life is freely offered to all by *faith*. The two loaves of wheat which were baked with *leaven* represented *Jews* and *Gentiles*. Both were stained with sin and required a Messiah to forgive those sins. What a beautiful type of New Covenant salvation. Both Jews and Gentiles deserve eternal damnation, but both are heirs to the promise through our Lord Jesus Christ.

The Feast of Shavuot is the 4th and last of the four Spring Feasts. Each was a *Moed* or a *rehearsal* of something which would happen in the distant future. Jesus Christ *exactly* satisfied each Spring Feast in His 1st advent, and there is no reason to not believe that He will satisfy the 3 Fall Feasts in His 2nd advent. After the Feast of Shavuot, there is a long growing season between Sivan 8 in the Spring and the *Feast of Trumpets* on Tishri 1 in the Fall. This long growing season is the maturation of the precious wheat. This is representative of the *Church Age* during which the full Body of Christ will be built of Jews and Gentiles alike (The two loaves baked with Wheat and Leaven). We will now see that the Wheat Harvest of New Covenant Christians will take place on some future Tishri 1.

Nisan 14	Nisan 15 To Nisan 21	On the Only Sunday Which Falls During the Feast of Unleavened Bread	50 day Count from only Sunday During Feast of Unleavened Bread
Passover	Unleavened Bread	Firstfruits	Pentecost
Exodus 12 Matthew 26:17-27 Leviticus 23:5	Leviticus 23:6-8	Leviticus 23:9-14 Deuteronomy 26:1-11	Leviticus 23:15-22 Deuteronomy 16:10
Crucifixion	Burial	Resurrection	Holy Spirit
John 18:28 1 Corithians 5:7	John 6:47-51 Acts 2:29-32	1 Corinthians 15:20-23 James 1:18	Acts 1 & 2

All Four spring feasts Were Completely satisfied at the First Advent of Jesus Christ

Part III
The Fall Feasts of Israel

We have seen how Christ exactly fulfilled each of the four Spring Feasts of Israel at his *first coming*. It is not difficult at all to believe that He will also fulfill each of the last three Feasts of Israel at his *second coming*. It remains to be seen exactly when this will be accomplished, but the prophetic fulfillment and relevance of each feast can be determined. The last three Feasts are partially concealed; and of course, hindsight in studying the first four Feasts is always better than foresight. Since all of the Feasts are Jewish in nature, we would be wise to examine what Jewish tradition has to say about the last three Feasts. In doing so, we will unveil a complete understanding of how we might expect this Age of Grace to come to an end. If Christ is going to satisfy the last three Feasts at his *Second Advent*, we can say with certainty that this will come to pass at the end of Daniel's last and 70th week (Daniel 9: 24-27, Phillips, *The Daniel 70 Week Prophecy: Cornerstone of all Prophecy*). The events we will describe can only occur when Christ returns to Rapture all of the saints, defeat Satan his followers at the Battle of Armageddon, celebrate and initiate the new 1000-year Millennial Kingdom and set up His throne in Jerusalem. The three Fall Feasts of Israel are:

(1) ***The Feast of Rosh Hashanah*** (*Feast of Trumpets*) **Tishri 1**
(2) ***The Feast of Yom Kippur*** (*Feast of Yom Teruah*) **Tishri 10**
(3) ***The Feast of Tabernacles*** (*Feast of Booths*) **Tishri 15-22**

The relative position of each Feast is shown in the diagram on the next page.

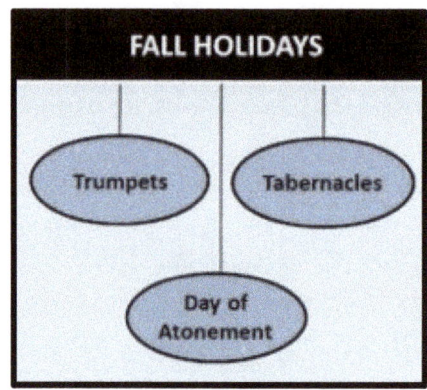

The three Fall Feasts all occur in the Jewish month of *Tishri*. Tishri is the first month of the *Jewish Civil Calendar,* and the seventh month of the *Jewish religious calendar*. All three Feasts will occur in a 22-day period of time in one of the Gregorian calendar months of September or October. Like the Spring festivals, they are closely aligned and associated with the agricultural cycle. The month of *Nisan* brings forth the new crop of *barley*. The month of *Tishri* ushers in the final harvest of *wheat*, corn, grapes and figs. Both the Spring and Fall festivals require rain to bring the precious fruit of the earth into full maturity.

Therefore, be patient, brethren, until the coming of the Lord. See how the farmer waits for the precious fruit of the earth, waiting patiently for it until it receives the early and the latter rain   James 5:7

The *early rains* fell on the newborn body of Christ on the day of Pentecost in 30 AD. We have been patiently waiting for the *latter rains* to Fall when Christ returns for His second advent. As previously noted, the Feasts represent both historical and spiritual significance. Historically they represent significant events that occurred when God chose Moses to lead His people out of Egyptian bondage. Spiritually, each feast is a *rehearsal* or an *appointment* that God has made for Jesus Christ at His second advent.

There is an interesting correlation between the civil and the religious calendar. The civil calendar starts in September or October on Tishri 1. This is said to be the birthday of the creation of the world, and the day on which Abraham was born. It is also when the wheat crop came to fullness and was dedicated to the Lord. When God liberated the Nation of Israel and Moses led them out of Egypt, God told Moses that that month Nisan would be the 1st month of the year to memorialize their freedom. This did not change the calendar in any way, it just renumbered the months of the year. The *religious* calendar begins in the month of March/April on Nisan 1. Nisan 1 is when the *barley* crop was coming into maturity and the wheat crop was starting to grow. The *Civil* calendar started on Tishri 1 which since the Exodus is the 7th month. For those who recognize the vicarious sacrifice of Jesus Christ on Nisan 14, the promise of resurrection from the dead and the gift of the Holy Spirit to every believer, the month of Nisan represents new beginnings in their spiritual relationship with Jesus Christ, and the month of Tishri the fulfillment of promises to both the Jews and Gentiles.

As we have already observed, there are almost 120 days between the *Feast of Pentecost* and the *Feast of Rosh Hashanah*. Physically, this is the long period of time when the Barley crop will mature and then start to be harvested on the Feast of Firstfruits. The more precious wheat crop will spring from the ear, mature, and grow between Nisan 1 and Tishri 1. Ten days later on Tishri 10 the *Feast of Yom Kippur* is celebrated. Five days after the Feast of Yom Kippur takes place, the *Feast of Tabernacles* will be observed (Tishri 15-22). The Feast of Tabernacles serve to remember how the children of Israel slept in tents (Tabernacles) during the 40-year exodus. It is a joyous feast that is to also celebrate the future redemption of all Jews and inheritance of the Promised Land. This will come to pass following the Last Feast of Tabernacles and the 1000-year Millennial Kingdom begins. The Feast of Yom Kippur connects the 5th Feast (Feast of Trumpets) and 7th Feast (Feast of Tabernacles) of Israel.

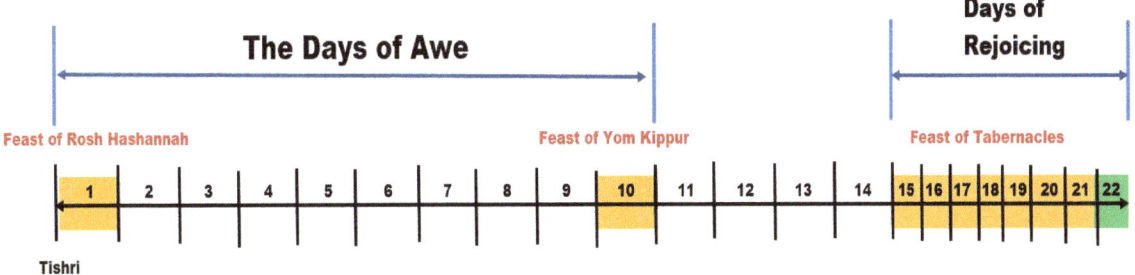

The 10 days which are between the Feast of Rosh Hashanah (Feast of Trumpets) and the Feast of Yom Kippur are called the *Days of Awe*. The Feast of Yom Kippur is the holiest day of the Hebrew year. The wheat which springs forth, matures and grows to harvest between the Spring Feast of Yom Teruah (Pentecost) and the Feast of Trumpets is a shadow and type of the *Church Age*. The precious wheat crop is a type of the *Body of Christ* or the *Born-again believers*. The body of Christ is growing, and one day God will declare that the harvest (*Rapture of the Saints*) has come. We will show that this is expected to occur on some future *Feast of Trumpets*.

Christians will not be surprised when the **war in the heavenlies** is fought (Revelation 12) and Satan is cast down to the earth. At that time, all will know that the great tribulation period has begun. It is a fallacy that believers will not know when the end is approaching (Matthew 24: 5-8). The European theatre will unite under a 10-nation confederacy, a peace treaty between these nations and Israel will be signed (the Covenant of Death), a new Jewish temple will be built in Jerusalem and a gifted orator/ military leader will arise *among* the 10-nation European confederacy. He will supernaturally rise against 3 nations and defeat them in battle (Daniel 8). He will then assume control of the new 7 nation confederacy as dictator (Daniel 11: 36-45). All of this will precede the heavenly battle described in Revelation 12: 7-8.

There will be plenty of heavenly and earthly signs for those who are watching (Matthew 24: 4-15, Revelation 6). It is certainly true that only God will know when the tribulation period will begin and on what calendar day the church age will end, but Paul in his first letter to the Thessalonians assured them that while the end will come suddenly, they were not to be unaware of what is about to happen. If this was true then, it is true now.

But concerning the times and the seasons, brethren, you have no need that I should write to you. For you yourselves know perfectly that the Day of the Lord so comes as a thief in the night. For when they say "peace and safety" then sudden destruction comes upon them, as labor pains upon a pregnant woman. And they shall not escape. But you, brethren, are not in darkness, so that this day should overtake you as a thief.   I Thessalonians 5:1-4

Notice that the apostle Paul is not denying that the Day of the Lord will come suddenly and bring destruction, but he emphatically and clearly assures them that they will not be surprised. Why would Paul assure them (and us) of this if it is not true?

One thing should be pointed out which is highly relevant to our study of the Fall feasts: In the Jewish mind, *Rosh Hashanah*, *Yom Kippur* and *Tabernacles* are separate Feasts but the Jews consider this time of year to form one season containing the three Feasts, just as the first four Spring Feasts were collectively called Passover. They will all be in the Jewish month of Tishri.

Feast of Rosh Hashanah (Trumpets)

Speak unto the children of Israel, saying, In the seventh month, in the first day of the month, shall ye have a sabbath, a memorial of blowing of trumpets, a holy convocation   Leviticus 23:24

The Feast of Rosh Hashana (Feast of Trumpets) is the least understood of all the 7 Jewish Feasts. It is to be a Holy Convocation which starts with the sound of a ram's horn called the *shofar*. It begins a 10-day period (Tishri 1-Tishri 10) which is one of penitence and repentance. These 10 days (inclusive) start on the Feast of Trumpets and end on the Feast of Yom Kippur. These days are called the *Days of Awe*.

The 10 Days of Awe are when each person is to confess their sins to God and seek to make things right with those they have sinned against physically or socially. Prophetically, the *Feast of Trumpets* is when the *Rapture* will take place; the *Battle of Armageddon* will take place on the *Feast of Yom Kippur* and the *Feast of Tabernacles* will usher in the

1000-year *Millennial Kingdom*. The Feast of Tabernacles (Sukkot) is the last of the 7 Holy convocations, and it is to commemorate how the Children of Israel slept in tents during their 49 years of wandering in the Deserts of Sinai. The Feast of Tabernacles is a feast of joyous celebration every year by the Jews. The following events are taught to occur on the last *Feast of Trumpets*.

- ➢ The long-awaited Messiah of Israel will finally come on that day,
- ➢ The dead will be raised and given a body just like that of Adam and Eve before the Fall
- ➢ The earth will be restored to its former Edenic state,
- ➢ All men will be judged at this time
- ➢ The Messiah who will save Israel will be installed as King of the Jews with the sound of the last trump
- ➢ The Wedding Feast of the Messiah will take place

The coronation of the Jewish Messiah as King of the Jews and the resurrection of King David who will rule and reign with the Messiah for 1000 years will be announced by the blast of a shofar at the last trump.

At the last Feast of Trumpets, the Messiah will not only be inaugurated as King, but he will also renew His ancient marriage vow to the adulterous Jews as his bride. According to the Holy Bible, *the commonwealth of Israel* is the bride of the bridegroom (Messiah). God is described in the Old Testament as married to Israel and Judah (Jeremiah 2:2, Isaiah 54: 5-8, Jeremiah 3: 10-14), and in the New Testament the church is described as the Bride of Christ (Ephesians 5: 25-27, II Corinthians 11:2, Revelation 7:9).

The marriage of God to Israel ended in a separation because of her adulterous behavior with foreign Gods and foreign women. Israel became Jehovah's *Wife* in the ceremony at the foot of Mt. Sinai (Exodus 19) when God gave Moses the Law and Israel said: *Yes*. The solemn, binding nature of this covenant was ratified by the blood of the covenant (Exodus 24: 3-8, Hebrews 9: 18-21). Israel was (repeatedly) an unfaithful, adulterous wife and was thus disowned by Jehovah

Deuteronomy 29: 25-28), but will she will one day in the future repent (Zachariah 12: 10-14) and be restored (Isaiah 62: 4, 5).

The Feast of Trumpets is also intimately connected to a 40-day period of time which begins on Elul 1 and ends on Tishri 10 (Feast of Yom Kippur).

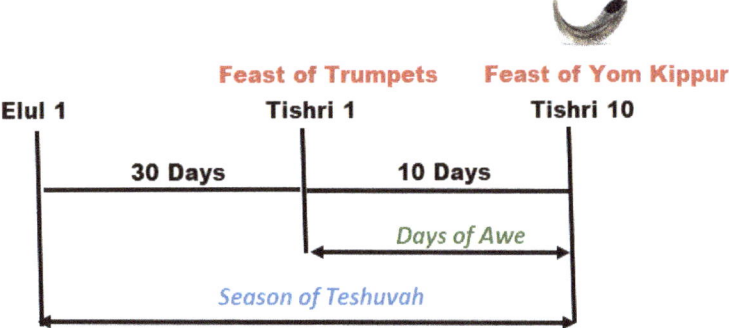

The 30-days between Elul 1 and Tishri 10 represent a call for repentance of each Jew. The Rabbi's teach that all men are inherently evil and prone to sin. Man is born with a tendency to sin because each inherits the sin nature from Adam. Each year, the 30 days leading up to the Feast of Teshuvah (Feast of Trumpets) is a time of introspection and examination. The 40 days between Elul 1 and Tishri 10 can be divided into four separate parts.

1. The 30-days in the month of Elul
2. The day of Rosh Hashanah
3. The 10-days between Rosh Hasanah and Yom Kippur
4. The day of Yom Kippur

According to Jewish tradition, the *final Feast of Trumpets* (Feast of Rosh Hashanah) will be initiated by the blast of a *shofar*. The *shofar* is not a normal horn, but is said to have been reserved for this special occasion since the *binding of Isaac*. Recall that God commanded Abraham to sacrifice his only son of promise, Isaac. As Abraham raised his knife to kill his son, God stayed his hand and delivered a ram as the substitute sacrifice. The ram was to be burned completely as a *burnt offering*. The only thing left was the two ram's horns. The *first horn* was said to have been blown on Mt. Sinai when the law was given; the *second horn* is reserved for the *last trump* at the last Feast of Rosh Hashanah (Trumpets). The 40-day season which begins on Elul 1 and ends on Tishri 10 is called *Teshuvah*. The Feast of Trumpets is held 30 days into the season of *Teshuvah* on Tishri 1. It is relevant to note that every morning during the month of Elul, a trumpet is sounded to warn all the people that the time has come to repent of their sins and return to God. Ask any orthodox Jew what the *last trump* means in relation to the ancient Feasts of Israel, and he will immediately respond that the last trump is the *shofar*, which will be blown at the last Feast of Rosh Hashanah.

On the last Feast of Trumpets, it is taught that there are several books which will be opened. The first is the **Book of Remembrance**.

Then they that fear the Lord spoke often to one another: and the Lord hearkened, and heard it, and a Book of Remembrance was written before him for them that feared the Lord, and that thought upon his name   Malachi 3:16

The second is actually *three sets of books*. Those who have committed to God and turned to righteousness are written in the *Book of the Righteous* or the **Book of Life** for the coming year. All other people are then divided into two groups. The first group is written into a book called the *Book of Rashim*, or the *Book of the Totally Wicked* (Daniel 12: 1-2). These are those who have totally rejected God and would not turn away from unrighteousness. The third or *last book* contains the names of those still alive who are not yet judged to be totally wicked, but have not fully repented and returned to God. The decision of where a person's name will be inscribed on Tishri 1 is preceded by repentance activities on the last day of Elul. That day is called *Erev Rosh Hashanah*. Orthodox Jews will be purified in a *Mikveh* or ritual bathing ceremony. It is also a tradition that during this time each male Jew will greet one another with the salutation: *May your name be inscribed in the Book of Life for another year.*

Those people whose names are not inscribed in the *Book of Life* on Tishri 1 will have *ten more days* before their fate is sealed. These 10 days are called the *Days of Awe,* and they are the days between Nisan 1 and Nisan 10 (Inclusive count). The *Feast of Yom Kippur* occurs on only one day: Nisan 10. For this reason, the Feast of Yom Kippur is called the *Day of Judgment*. If anyone does not repent and turn away from sin by Tishri 10, their names will not be inscribed in the **Book of Life** for the coming year.

Messianic Application

If all of this sounds familiar to you, then it should. It is generally believed by those who have studied the 7 Feasts of Israel that on the Feast of Trumpets, at the *last trump*, the *rapture* of the church will occur and the dead in Christ will rise to meet Christ in the air. These saints will receive their new, glorified, eternal bodies (Revelation 11:15-18). This will then initiate the **Marriage of the Lamb** (Revelation 19:7). The saints who are raptured and raised from the dead are those who have had their names inscribed in the **Lamb's Book of Life** (Revelation 21:27).

When the Body of Christ is resurrected and raptured on Tishri 1, they will meet Jesus Christ in the air. The rapture will be initiated by a *shout* and the *sound of a trumpet* (I Thessalonians 4: 16-18) …. the *last trumpet* (I Corinthians 15: 51-53). After the rapture occurs, the people who are left alive and still remain are all unbelievers; those whose names are not inscribed in the Lambs Book of Life. The 10 days between the Feast of Trumpets and the Feast of Yom Kippur will be the *last chance* for all who remain after the rapture to escape eternal damnation. Those who reach the next feast, the *Feast of Yom Kippur*, without accepting Christ as their savior will be cast into the *bottomless pit* for 1000 years, and after the millennial kingdom they will be raised and judged at the *Great White Throne Judgment*; they will then be cast into the *lake of burning fire* (Revelation 20:13). There is a disagreement among Christians concerning the Lake of Burning fire and eternal punishment of those who die without accepting Jesus Chrit as their Lord and savior. Some believe that God is a merciful God and would not enforce eternal punishment upon anyone. Others say that the choice was clear to each individual: Receive the free gift of eternal life by faith or receive eternal punishment for lack of faith. The entire disagreement should be settled by the source of all truth…. the Holy Scriptures. Revelation 20:15 specifically says that those who will not believe are cast into the *Lake of Burning Fire*. Jesus Christ said in Matthew 25:46 that the punishment of unbelievers is eternal. It is a sad thing, but failure of anyone to accept Jesus Christ as their personal Savior before they die is a personal, irrevocable decision. There is no second chance.

The Jewish rabbis teach that on some future Feast of Trumpets a Wedding ceremony will take place.

In the Old Testament God chose Israel to be His special people.

[6] *For thou art an holy people unto the LORD thy God: the LORD thy God hath chosen thee to be a special people unto himself, above all people that are upon the face of the earth.*
[7] *The LORD did not set his love upon you, nor choose you, because ye were more in number than any people; for ye were the fewest of all people:*
[8] *But because the LORD loved you, and because he would keep the oath which he had sworn unto your fathers, hath the LORD brought you out with a mighty hand, and redeemed you out of the house of bondmen, from the hand of Pharaoh king of Egypt.*   Deuteronomy 7: 6-8

God loved His chosen people so much that He chose them to be His Eternal bride.

[18] *And in that day will I make a covenant for them with the beasts of the field, and with the fowls of heaven, and with the creeping things of the ground: and I will break the bow and the sword and the battle out of the earth, and will make them to lie down safely. And I will betroth thee unto*

[19] *me forever; yea,* **I will betroth thee unto me** *in righteousness, and in judgment, and in lovingkindness, and in mercies*   Hosea 2: 18-19

[31] *Behold, the days come, saith the LORD, that I will make a new covenant with the house of Israel, and with the house of Judah:*
[32] *Not according to the covenant that I made with their fathers in the day that I took them by the hand to bring them out of the land of Egypt; which my covenant they brake,* **although I was a husband unto them**, *saith the LORD:*   Jeremiah 31: 31-32

Israel was chosen to be the Bride of God, but Satan caused sin, corruption and adulatory to lead their lives. They went hoaring after strange Idols, strange Gods, and strange women. In His anger, God turned His back upon them for a season. God will yet forgive His bride of their adulterous and unfaithful acts and He will reconcile them to Himself for all eternity.

[33] *But this shall be the covenant that I will make with the house of Israel; After those days, saith the LORD, I will put my law in their inward parts, and write it in their hearts; and will be their God, and they shall be my people.*
[34] *And they shall teach no more every man his neighbor, and every man his brother, saying, Know the LORD: for they shall all know me, from the least of them unto the greatest of them, saith the LORD; for I will forgive their iniquity, and I will remember their sin no more.*
Jeremiah 31: 33-34

[6] *The LORD said also unto me in the days of Josiah the king, Hast thou seen that which backsliding Israel hath done? she is gone up upon every high mountain and under every green tree, and there hath played the harlot.*
[7] *And I said after she had done all these things, Turn thou unto me.*

But she returned not. And her treacherous sister Judah saw it.

[8] And I saw, when for all the causes whereby backsliding Israel committed adultery I had put her away, and given her a bill of divorce; yet her treacherous sister Judah feared not, but went and played the harlot also.

[9] And it came to pass through the lightness of her whoredom, that she defiled the land, and committed adultery with stones and with stocks.

[10] And yet for all this her treacherous sister Judah hath not turned unto me with her whole heart, but feignedly, saith the LORD.

[11] And the LORD said unto me, The backsliding Israel hath justified herself more than treacherous Judah.

Jeremiah 3: 6-11

*[12] Go and proclaim these words toward the north, and say***, Return, thou backsliding Israel, saith the LORD; and I will not cause mine anger to fall upon you: for I am merciful, saith the LORD, and I will not keep anger forever.***

[13] Only acknowledge thine iniquity, that thou hast transgressed against the LORD thy God, and hast scattered thy ways to the strangers under every green tree, and ye have not obeyed my voice, saith the LORD.

[14] Turn, O backsliding children, saith the LORD; for I am married unto you: and I will take you one of a city, and two of a family, and I will bring you to Zion:

[15] And I will give you pastors according to mine heart, which shall feed you with knowledge and understanding.

[16] And it shall come to pass, when ye be multiplied and increased in the land, in those days, saith the LORD, they shall say no more, The ark of the covenant of the LORD: neither shall it come to mind: neither shall they remember it; neither shall they visit it; neither shall that be done any more.

[17] At that time they shall call Jerusalem the throne of the LORD; and all the nations shall be gathered unto it, to the name of the LORD, to Jerusalem: neither shall they walk any more after the imagination of their evil heart.

[18] In those days the house of Judah shall walk with the house of Israel, and they shall come together out of the land of the north to the land that I have given for an inheritance unto your fathers.   Jeremiah 3: 12-18

There is yet another group of people to recognize: they are those who have missed the rapture and have accepted Christ as their Savior during the 10 days of repentance. This group is entirely hidden from Jewish teachings since they do not yet recognize Christ as Messiah and King. The scriptures are not clear as to their disposition. It is assumed that this group will pass into the millennial kingdom with the 144,000 that were sealed in Revelation 7: 1-8. The 144,000 from 12 tribes of Israel were sealed from the Wrath of God which are the *Seven bowl judgments,* poured out upon the earth between Nisan 1 and Nisan 10 (Revelation 15:1, Revelation 16:1).

Both our view of end-time events and the Jewish view of their salvation are perfectly aligned and consistent. The only difference is that the Jewish nation as a whole has been *blinded in part* until the scales are removed from their eyes and they can see. The Jewish nation as a whole is looking for their messiah to arise and save them; their conquering king is called *Messiah Ben David*, not Jesus Christ.

But even if our gospel is veiled, it is veiled to those who are perishing. Whose minds the god of this age has blinded, who do not believe, lest the light of the gospel of the glory of Christ, who is the image of God should shine upon them   II Corinthians 4: 3-4

The period of time between Tishri 1 (Feast of Trumpets) and Tishri 10 (Feast of Yom Kippur) has been identified by Phillips, *A New Pre-Wrath*

Rapture Theory as the last chance that Jews or Gentiles alike to accept Jesus Christ as their Lord and Savior. It is during these 10 days that the Jews will finally turn to Jesus Christ as their long-awaited Messiah

[25] For I would not, brethren, that ye should be ignorant of this mystery, lest ye should be wise in your own conceits; that blindness in part is happened to Israel, until the fulness of the Gentiles be come in. [26] And so all Israel shall be saved: as it is written, There shall come out of Sion the Deliverer, and shall turn away ungodliness from Jacob: [27] For this is my covenant unto them, when I shall take away their sins
Romans 11: 25-27

A common misconception among Christians is that the Jews (Old Testament) did not believe in a resurrection of the dead. This is not true. All orthodox Jews today believe that their ancestors will be resurrected from the dead. The prophet Daniel had no concept of Jesus Christ or of the body of Christ, but he wrote that there would be a resurrection.

[1] And at that time shall Michael stand up, the great prince which stands for the children of thy people: and there shall be a time of trouble, such as never was since there was a nation even to that same time: and at that time thy people shall be delivered, every one that shall be found written in the book (Book of life)
[2] And many of them that sleep in the dust of the earth shall awake, some to everlasting life, and some to shame and everlasting contempt
Daniel 12: 1-2

The Apostle John wrote of the same thing concerning all born-again believers and all unbelievers.

And shall come forth; they that have done good, unto the resurrection of life; and they that have done evil, unto the resurrection of damnation
John 5:29

As with many Old Testament prophecies, there is a near-far perspective because the Church age was unknown to all Old Testament prophets. The prophetic revelation of Daniel in Daniel 12: 1-2 is pointing to two different points in time, both yet future: (1) Those (Jews) who will awake to everlasting *life* will be those who have their name inscribed in the *Book of Life.* They will be resurrected at the last trump (rapture) with all true believers. Those who awake to *everlasting contempt* will not awake until the end of the Millennial Kingdom and will be judged at the *Great White Throne Judgment.* By the 1st century AD, the subject of resurrection had become a highly debated topic. The Pharisees believed and taught that there would be a resurrection, while the Sadducees did not believe in a resurrection. There should have been no controversy if the Sadducees had carefully studied the Old Testament.

Thy dead men shall live, together with my dead body shall they arise. Awake and sing, ye that dwell in dust: for thy dew is as the dew of herbs, and the earth shall cast out the dead　　　　Isaiah 26:19

It is difficult to understand why the Pharisees would not believe in a resurrection. If there is no resurrection, then the Prophet Daniel and the prophet Isaiah are both wrong; and this would be heresy. If there is no resurrection of dead Jews, what hope does any Jew have of living for eternity? This is the problem with both Christians and Jews today that reject resurrection. If there is no resurrection, then there is no life after death and the few years that man spends here on earth is all that can be expected. If there is no resurrection of the righteous dead for eternal rewards and a resurrection of unrighteous dead for eternal punishment, what difference does it make if there is a righteous Book of Judgment, a Book of Deeds or a Book of Life? Simply eat, drink, sin and be merry; for tomorrow death will simply terminate existence.

It is written in the Jewish Talmud that the resurrection of the dead will take place on some future Rosh Hasannah. It is taught that when the resurrection takes place, the last *shofar* (Ram's Horn) will be blown. It is interesting that the beliefs of devout Jews closely parallel the mystery that Paul revealed to the New Jewish converts in I Thessalonians 4: 13-18 and II Thessalonians 2: 1-3.

The Royal Coronation

Another belief the Jews hold concerning what will occur on the Feast of Trumpets is one of a *Royal Coronation*. The coronation of their long-awaited Messiah will occur on the same day as the resurrection. Another name for this day is Yom HaKeseh, *the Day of Concealment* or the *Hidden Day.* When Christians accept Jesus Christ as their Lord and Savior; God forgives, *hides* and *conceals* our sins from His memory.

Rapture of the Saints

The reward of Rapture or resurrection when Jesus Christ arrives in the air is currently hidden from all but a remnant of Messianic Jews.

[16] *This is the covenant that I will make with them after those days, saith the Lord, I will put my laws into their hearts, and in their minds will I write them;*
[17] *And their sins and iniquities will I remember no more*
Hebrews 10: 16-17

The year and day of the week which the rapture will take place cannot be determined: Only God knows (Matthew 24:36). However, this does not mean that the time and season cannot be known. Biblical Scholars who study the 7 Feasts of Israel believe that the Rapture of all true believers will take place on some future *Feast of Trumpets*.

In Colossians 2: 16-17, the Apostle Paul refers to each Festival as being a *rehearsal* or a *Moed* of the coming Messiah at an *appointed time*.

[16] Let no man therefore judge you in meat, or in drink, or in respect of a holy day, or of the new moon, or of the sabbath days:
[17] Which are a shadow of things to come; but the body is of Christ
    Colossians 2:16-17

Most if not all of the Biblical Scholars who study the 7 Feasts of Israel agree that the Feast of Trumpets holds the key to when an event called the *Rapture* will occur. Most that we know of the Rapture was a Mystery until it was explained by the Apostle Paul.

[13] But I would not have you to be ignorant, brethren, concerning them which are asleep, that ye sorrow not, even as others which have no hope.
*[14] For **if we believe that Jesus died and rose again**, even so them also which sleep in Jesus will God bring with him.*
*[15] For this we say unto you by the word of the Lord, that **we which are alive and remain unto the coming of the Lord shall not prevent them which are asleep.***
*[16] **For the Lord himself shall descend from heaven** with a shout, with the **voice of the archangel**, and with the **trump of God**: and the dead in Christ shall rise first:*
*[17] Then we which are alive and remain shall be caught up together with them in the clouds, to meet the Lord in the air: and **so shall we ever be with the Lord***   I Thessalonians 4: 13-17

*[51] Behold, I shew you a **mystery**; We shall not all sleep, but we shall all be changed,*
*[52] **In a moment**, in the twinkling of an eye, **at the last trump**: for the trumpet shall sound, and the dead shall be raised incorruptible, and we shall be changed.*
*[53] For this **corruptible must put on incorruption**, and this **mortal must put on immortality.***
[54] So when this corruptible shall have put on incorruption, and this

mortal shall have put on immortality, then shall be brought to pass the saying that is written, Death is swallowed up in victory
I Corinthians 15: 51-54

Paul is very clear that the blessed hope of every Christian is that whether alive or dead, Christ will one day return to gather all true believers to be with Him forever. Our Lord and Savior Jesus Christ will return in the air: The *dead* will be raised *first* and *then* those *who remain alive* will ascend to meet Christ. There will be a *shout* from an archangel and then a *trumpet will sound*. We will then all be changed and given a new, incorruptible body.

This will all take place for certain at some day in the future when the *Body of Christ* has been completed. This will happen at the *Last Trump*, but can we be more specific about when this will happen? The *words of Jesus Christ* provide a clue.

[29] ***Immediately after the tribulation of those days*** *shall the sun be darkened, and the moon shall not give her light, and the stars shall fall from heaven, and the powers of the heavens shall be shaken:*
[30] *And **then shall appear** the sign of **the Son of man** in heaven: and then shall all the tribes of the earth mourn, and **they shall see the Son of man coming** in the clouds of heaven with power and great glory.*
[31] *And he shall **send his angels** with a great **sound of a trumpet**, and they shall gather together his elect from the four winds, from one end of heaven to the other*   Matthew 24: 29-31

There can be no doubt that Jesus Christ is describing the same event that Paul is describing in the previous verses. It is surprising to this author that the words of Christ have been completely ignored when theologians discuss the rapture. Jesus Christ was very specific as to when the rapture would take place: ***Immediately after the tribulation of those days, they shall see the Son of man coming in the clouds of heaven with power and great glory.*** Nothing could be clearer……. The rapture will ***not*** be a pre-tribulation rapture as most teach: It will take place ***after*** the

Tribulation of those days. Actually, other words spoken by Jesus Christ reveal that toward the end of the 3.5 years of Satanic tribulation, that: *except those days should be shortened, there should no flesh be saved: but for the elect's sake those days shall be shortened* (Matthew 24:22). The Great tribulation of 3.5 years will not be shortened, but the *elect* will not have to endure the *Wrath of God* (Romans 1:18, Romans 5:9, Colossians 3:6, I Thessalonians 1:10, I Thessalonians 5:9). So: *What is the Wrath of God?* This is very Clear: The Wrath of God is the 7 Bowl/vial judgments (Revelation 15:1, Revelation 16:1, Phillips, *The Wrath of God*). Rapture at the 7th Trump shortens the Tribulation period by 10 days, and immediately precedes the 7 Bowl Judgments. This is shown in a new *Pre-Wrath* Theory fully developed in Phillips, *A New Pre-Wrath Rapture Theory*. All Christians who are still alive at the *last trump* (some future Feast of Trumpets), will not have to go through the 7 Bowl Judgments. This forms the basis of what I propose is a new Pre-Wrath Rapture Theory where all Christians will be raptured out at the 7th Trumpet. This is consistent with the Jewish belief that all Jews who have their name in a Book of Life will be rewarded on the last Feast of Trumpets.

Jesus also referred to the *rapture* in Matthew 24:31 as being launched by a *sound of a trumpet.* Paul has added that the rapture will be preceded by a *trumpet call of God* (I Thessalonians 4:16). In I Corinthians, he is specific about *which* trump.

[51] *Behold, I shew you a mystery; We shall not all sleep, but we shall all be changed,*
[52] *In a moment, in the twinkling of an eye, at the **last trump**: for the trumpet shall sound, and the dead shall be raised incorruptible, and we shall be* changed   I Corinthians 15: 51-52

Paul writes that **we will all be changed**, whether we are alive or dead, at the **last trump**. Now that is fairly specific, but: *When would the **last trump** be sounded?* Those who casually read I Corinthians 15:52 and have also read the Book of Revelation, are tempted to assume that since there are 7 trumpets which will be blown by angels in the Book of Revelation, and that the 7th trumpet is the last. Hence, one might conclude that the rapture will occur as the 7th trumpet sounds. This is certainly true, but it is not the real reason. The term ***last trump*** is a Jewish eschatological term always connected to the last *Feast of Rosh Hashanah* or the *Feast of Trumpets*...which will occur on some future Tishri 1. As previously discussed, Jewish people see Rosh Hashanah (Feast of Trumpets) as the last day. This is because they do not believe that the *Rapture* will be by Jesus Christ *in the air*, and the final 10 days between the final Feast of Trumpets and the final day of Yom Kippur will be the last 10-day period during which all Jews and Gentiles who remain can find salvation. As this final 10-day period draws to an end, all Jews who still remain alive will finally recognize Jesus Christ as their long-awaited Messiah.

[25] *For I would not, brethren, that ye should be ignorant of this mystery, lest ye should be wise in your own conceits; that blindness in part is happened to Israel, until the fulness of the Gentiles be come in.*
[26] *And so all Israel shall be saved: as it is written, There shall come out of Sion the Deliverer, and shall turn away ungodliness from Jacob:*
[27] *For this is my covenant unto them, when I shall take away their sins.*
[28] *As concerning the gospel, they are enemies for your sakes: but as touching the election, they are beloved for the fathers' sakes*
Romans 11: 25-28

The Last Trump

There are 30 days of blowing the trumpet on each day *preceding* Tishri 1. A ***last trump*** is blown on the Feast of Trumpets. But there is also a trumpet blown on Tishri 10, so again.... *When is the last trumpet?* Here we must dig deeper into Jewish Rabbinical teachings. According to the ancient Jewish rabbis and teachers, the ***last trump*** is related to the **Binding of Isaac**. Recall that Abraham was called by God to sacrifice his son Isaac, and he went up onto a mountain to do so. Ancient teachings say that Abraham went to where the **Dome of the Rock** now stands. He built an altar of stones and just as he was about to kill his son, God stayed his hand and produced a ***ram*** for a suitable sacrifice. This ram was offered as a ***burnt offering*** to the Lord and was totally consumed by fire. The only thing that survived was the two ram's horns. Tradition holds that the first horn was blown by God himself when the Law was given to Moses and the people at Mt. Sinai. The second horn…. The second and ***last horn***…. is to be blown at a future **Feast of Rosh Hashanah** (Feast of Trumpets). The Feast of Trumpets is also called *Yom Teruah* or the *Day of Awakening Blast*. The *awakening blast* on some future Feast of Rosh Hashanah refers to a Jewish belief that the dead will be raised on this day. The resurrection of all Jews on Rosh Hashanah is widely taught and believed by the Jewish Rabbis, and by the Jewish Old Testament prophets.

The fact that the last trump in the Book of Revelation is the last in a series of 7 does not fully justify that the Rapture of all living saints and the resurrection of all dead saints will occur when the 7th trumpet sounds, but supported by Jewish beliefs it is a distinct and logical possibility. The *Jewish* beliefs concerning the *last trump* are largely unknown to Western prophecy scholars who have not studied the *7 Feasts of Israel*.

The Bride of Christ

God has previously taken Israel for His bride, and Jesus Christ will take the body of Christ…...all Born-again believers…. as His bride. The apostle Paul wrote to the members of the Church in Corinth:

For I am jealous for you with godly jealousy. For I have betrothed you to one husband, that I may present you as a chaste virgin to Christ
II Corinthians 11:2

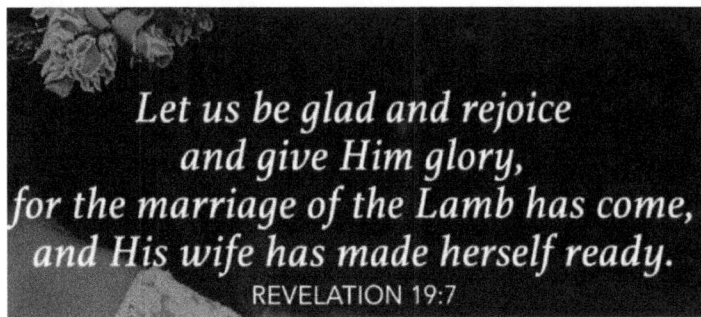

*And to her was granted that she should be arrayed in fine linen, clean and white: for the fine **linen is the righteousness of** saints* Revelation 19:8

Paul also reveals:

That he might present it to himself a glorious church, not having spot, or wrinkle, or any such thing; but that it should be holy and without blemish Ephesians 5:27

In order to fully understand how Jewish marriage customs are a type of the Marriage of the Lamb, it is necessary to review Jewish Marriage. When a young Jewish male finds a woman that He wishes to marry, he visits the house of his bride-to-be. He will carry with him three things: (1) A dowry which will be offered to the bride's family for the hand of their daughter. (2) a betrothal (marriage) contract of agreement and (3) a flaggard of wine. The suiter would meet with the father and the rest of the family and request that the maiden be married to him. The dowry is discussed, the marriage contract is laid out, and a glass of wine is poured. Once the proposition is discussed and agreed upon, the bride-to-be is called to the table and if all is settled then both will drink of the cup of wine. This signifies that the bride is now betrothed. Unlike Western marriage customs, this agreement is binding and as far as the father and the bride are concerned, she is now considered married even though the marriage ceremony has not taken place. The groom now leaves the house of the bride and returns to his own father to build a house for he and his bride. The groom proceeds to build a house for him and his bride. The house must be fully completed before the marriage can be consummated. The groom might be asked: *when will you return for your bride?* And he will answer: *When my father tells me to go and claim my bride. No one knows but my father.*

The bride is not completely ignorant of what is going on. In fact, she is fairly certain of when the groom will return and the marriage ceremony can take place. The bride has made herself ready, and as the time nears, she assembles all of her bridesmaids and invites them to her house, announcing: *Be prepared.* The groom with his entourage typically arrives at the house of his bride around midnight and announces: *I am here!* Of course, this is to be a surprise but those who watch and wait will know what is about to take place. The bride and her bridesmaids will arise and run to meet the husband. There are always those who have not prepared themselves and they will be left behind (Parable of wise and foolish virgins).

When the marriage ceremony is actually performed, a marriage agreement is witnessed and signed by both families. Following the official marriage ceremony, the couple immediately proceed to a special place called the *Chupah* which has been prepared for their honeymoon. Typically, the honeymoon lasts 5-7 days. The best man is assigned to guard the door of the chupah and after the marriage is consummated, a bloody piece of clothing is thrown out the door to show that the marriage has been consummated. The couple will then be called forth, and a week-long celebration is begun with joy and rejoicing.

It is strange and almost unbelievable that this marriage scenario can be almost directly applied to the Marriage of the Lamb to his betrothed wife (the church).
- Jesus Christ chose His wife before he was crucified
- At the Lords Last Supper, He affirmed His intentions with a glass of wine which was shared with His family (His disciples)
- He then went away to prepare a house for His bride (John 14: 1-2)
- He will return to claim His bride only when His father says He can (Matthew 24:36)
- The Church is anxiously awaiting His return

- The return of Jesus Christ in His 2cd advent will not be a surprise to those who watch and wait. But it will be a sudden surprise to those who are not ready (Parable of wise and Foolish Virgins)
- When the Father says: *Go......*Christ will return to claim His bride (Rapture of the Saints)
- The bride will be hidden in the *Chupah* for 10 days.

[1] *Gather yourselves together, yea, gather together, O nation not desired;*
[2] *Before the decree bring forth, before the day pass as the chaff, before the fierce anger of the LORD come upon you, before the **day of the LORD's anger** come upon you.*
[3] *Seek ye the LORD, all ye meek of the earth, which have wrought his judgment; seek righteousness, seek meekness: **it may be ye shall be hid in the day of the LORD's anger***
Zepeniah 2: 1-3

- The Bride of Christ will be hidden for a time (10 days) while the Wrath of God falls upon all unbelievers (The 7 Bowl Judgments, see Phillips, *The Day of Gods Wrath*.
- There will be a joyous and glorious wedding of the Lord after the earth has been purged of all unbelievers after the Battle of Armageddon.
- During the Feast of Tabernacles, a celebration will be held involving all true believers.
- The Old Testament Jews who died in faith will not be a part of the Bride of Christ: They are already married to God. They will be the Wedding Guests (John 3:29).
- The house which Jesus Christ built for His bride is the New Jerusalem (Revelation 21: 2-3)

This has only been a short examination of how the wedding ceremony of 1st century Jews parallels the wedding ceremony of the Bride of Christ. further details are left to the reader to discover on their own.

We have seen that God chose Israel as His special people, and that part of His intimate relationship with Israel is to choose her as His bride. The Lord married her and adorned her with presents and riches, but then Israel split into a Northern Kingdom (Israel) and a Southern Kingdom (Judah). The Northern Kingdom pursued adultery, idol worship and worldly goods. She forgot her marriage vows at Mt. Sinai, and became so wicked and unfaithful that the Lord finally let her go whoring. She would not repent, so the Lord allowed Assyria to completely annialate the Northern Kingdom (Josea 4: 16-19). The 10 Northern tribes vanished into history and were never heard from again. The southern Kingdom of Judah saw how God had ordained Assyria to conquer and destroy the Northern Kingdom of Israel, but without remorse or respect for God, they also fully apostatized. Finally, God had endured enough from her (Southern Kingdom of Judah), and He allowed Babylon to completely destroy His Holy temple and carry the Southern Kingdom into captivity for 70 years. Although God allowed Assyria and Babylon to completely destroy the 12 tribes of Israel, He is also a God of mercy and longsuffering. The Book of Hosea should be carefully studied. It is largely a story of how God will restore and love His chosen people (Hosea 2: 21-23).

- Hosea contrasts the unfaithful wives of Gomer and Hosea to that of His bride…. Israel
- Hosea detailed how the Lord judged Israel and punished her for unfaithfulness and adultery with foreign gods.
- The separation of His unfaithful and adulterous bride
- The ultimate restoration of Israel as His chosen bride.

One of the ways in which God proves His love for Israel is to describe Himself as their husband who has endured adultery, but will someday forgive her and take her back. *Your Maker is your husband— the LORD Almighty is his name.* (Isaiah 54:5; Jeremiah 31:32). *Return, thou backsliding Israel, saith the LORD; and I will not cause mine anger to fall upon you: for I am merciful, saith the LORD, and I will not keep anger forever* (Jeremiah 3:12).

The bride will be hidden in the chamber (Chupah) of God as He pours out the 7 Bowls of God's wrath upon all unbelievers. They will re-emerge from their wedding chamber and accompany Christ to the Battle of Armageddon.

[15] **Blow the trumpet** *in Zion, sanctify a fast, call a solemn assembly:* [16] *Gather the people, sanctify the congregation, assemble the elders, gather the children, and those that suck the breasts*: **let the bridegroom go forth of his chamber, and the bride out of her closet**
Joel 2: 15-16

Just as God chose Israel for His bride under the Old Testament economy, Jesus Christ will also choose His bride under the New Covenant. The complete New Testament body of Christ will be comprised of those who have trusted in Jesus Christ as their personal Savior and have received eternal life. Christ, the Bridegroom, has sacrificially and lovingly chosen the church to be His bride (Ephesians 5:25–27).

Just as there was a period in biblical times during which the bride and groom were separated until the wedding, so is the bride of Christ separated from her Bridegroom during the church age. Her responsibility during the betrothal period is to be faithful to Him (II Corinthians 11:2; Ephesians 5:24). At the *rapture,* the church will be united with the Bridegroom and the official "wedding ceremony" will take place and, the eternal union of Christ and His bride will be actualized (Revelation 19:7–9; 21:1-2). The Wedding supper of the Lamb will take place sometime during the Feast of Tabernacles (Revelation 19: 9-14).

The Feast of Yom Kippur (Yom Teruah)

Yom Kippur is generally regarded as the holiest day of the Jewish year. It terminates a 10-day period of introspection, self-examination and repentance during which each individual is judged to determine their status with God over the next Jewish Year. Recall that the name of each individual is recorded in one of two Holy Books: (1) The *Book of Life* and the (1) *Book of Death*. However, the names of most people will not be recorded in either book, but have a period of 10-days in which to determine their fate. According to the Talmud, God will open each of three books on Rosh Hashanah. If our deeds are good, he writes our names in the Book of Life. If our deeds are wicked, he writes our names in the Book of Death – but if our deeds fall somewhere in between, they are written in a third book. God suspends judgment on those whose names he writes in this book. Those people have ten days to change their hearts and lives. On Yom Kippur the fate of each individual is sealed. Evidence of a Book of Life can be found in Exodus and in the Book of Revelation (Revelation 20: 12,15). Moses descended Mt. Sinai with the 10-commandments which God had written on tablets of stone, and found that the Israelites had made idols of gold and silver and was worshipping the golden calf. Moses pleads for God's forgiveness. He asks God to blot out his name from the book God has written (Book of Life) if God will not forgive his people. This book is mentioned again in Psalms 69, in which the psalmist asks God to let the names of his adversaries be *blotted out of the book of the living*.

On Yom Kippur, the name of every living Jew is found written in one of these three books. The *Feast of Yom Kippur* is on Tishri 10, which is also known as the *Feast of Atonement*. This day is a *holy convocation* and it is also a day of *fasting*. It was being observed when Nadab and Abihu, the two sons of Aaron, filled a censor with *profane fire* and used it to offer up incense in the Holy Place (Numbers 3:4). Fire (coals) was not to be used at the Altar of Incense unless it came from the Brazen Altar. After their death, Aaron the high priest was told that he could not come before the Lord in the Holy of Holies without observing the strict laws put down by God (Leviticus 16).

The only day of the year that the high priest could come before God was on the *Day of Atonement*. On that day he would make a sacrifice for his sins, and then for the sins of the people. It was also on this day that two goats were chosen for a special offering to the Lord. One goat was for a sin offering unto the Lord, the other was to be led away into the wilderness and pushed over a high cliff outside of Jerusalem. This was called the *scapegoat*. The high priest would choose which goat would be the scapegoat by using the *Urim* and the *Thummin*. Once the scapegoat was chosen, a red scarlet cloth was tied around his horns. The high priest would place his hands on the scapegoat, symbolically transferring the sins of the people to that goat. The scapegoat was then led away to a high cliff outside of the city and pushed to its death, symbolically representing the *removal of sin from the people*. The other goat was then sacrificed and his blood caught in a bowl.

On Yom Kippur, the High Priest would wash and purify himself in a ritual bath and then make a burnt *sin offering* for his own sins. He would then place the coals of sacrifice upon the Alter of Incense which stood before the veil which separated the Holy Place from the Holy of Holies. The smoke would fill the Holy Place and the High Priest *alone* would enter into the Holy Place behind the veil. He would then come before the Ark of the Covenant and sprinkle the blood *seven times* on the *mercy seat*. The High Priest would then plead the sins of the people to God, who would come and dwell above the mercy seat in a cloud (Gaster). If the Lord would accept this act of atonement, the people could live another year without God executing permanent judgment (final atonement).

Messianic Application
This is clearly a picture of Jesus Christ. He was *the scapegoat* who was led outside the city to a place called Golgotha (Matthew 27:33, Mark 15:22, Luke 23:33, John 19:17) where He was nailed to a cross. Like the scapegoat, He took the sins of the world upon himself. *He who knew no sin became sin for us*. He was also the *sin offering* represented by the

second goat. His precious blood was shed for us; it was sprinkled on everyone from Adam to the Millennial kingdom, and He sprinkled it Himself before the throne of God for the sins of all mankind. Jesus was *both* the sacrifice and the one who offered the sacrifice. He is now our High Priest who continuously intercedes for us and He sits on the right-hand side of God the Father on His throne.

At his sacrificial death, the veil in the temple which separated man from God was rent in two, from top to bottom. This represented that there was no longer a separation of the people from God, but now by the blood of Jesus Christ we can boldly go before the Throne of God in the presence of Jesus Christ who intercedes for us. He is both our *redeemer* and our *High Priest*. In one person at one cross, Christ was both the scapegoat for all our sins and the blood offering to God. The writer of Hebrews spoke of the necessity for a blood sacrifice.

And almost all things are by the law purged with blood; and without shedding of blood is no remission   Hebrews 9:22

Now where remission of these is, there is no more offering for sin Hebrews 10:18

Jesus Christ was both the perfect sacrificial Lamb of God without spot or blemish, and he is also our eternal high priest since He ascended to glory on the Feast of Firstfruits. *The Sacrifice of bulls and goats could never forgive sins* (Hebrews 10:4); only the blood of Jesus Christ. It is sad how modern Jews have failed to recognize that Jesus Christ is the perfect and final sacrifice for all sins that they have always waited for. Salvation to both Jews and gentiles is now available by *faith*…...faith and nothing else.

The Battle of Armageddon

The *Feast of Yom Kippur* is when the most important battle will take place since time began. On the Feast of Yom Kippur (Tishri 10) Jesus Christ will fight the *Battle of Armageddon*.

On Tishri 10 (Jewish calendar) Christ will descend from heaven: His feet will land on the Mt. of Olives, and it will split the mountain into two parts…… so that half of the mountain will move toward the north and the other half toward the south. The Mt. of Olives is really not a mountain at all, but is a long ridge running North and South of Jerusalem and only rises 330 feet above Jerusalem.

After His resurrection, Jesus gave the Great Commission to His disciples and then **ascended to heaven** from the Mount of Olives (Acts 1:9-12). The place of His going will be the place of His coming. The prophet Zechariah foresaw the Second Coming of Christ (Zechariah 14: 1-4, 9).

The Battle of Armageddon will be fought at a place called the *Jezreel Valley*.  History records that 34 battles that have been fought at Jezreel Valley, sometimes called *Megiddo* over the past 4000 years.

To summarize: the Feast of Yom Kippur terminates a 40-day period called *Teshuvah*. It begins on the first day of the 12th Jewish month of the civil calendar called *Elul*. The 30 days in Elul which precedes the Feast of Trumpets is a time when all Jews are to repent of their sins so that their name will be inscribed in the *Book of Life*. As previously mentioned, the 10 days between the Feast of Trumpets on Tishri 1 and The Feast of Yom Kippur on Tishri 10 are known as the *Days of Repentance* or the *Days of Awe*.

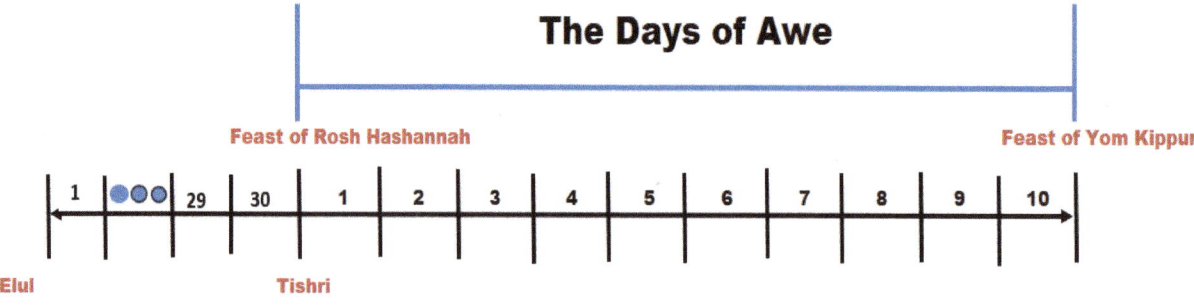

This 10-day period (inclusive) is the last chance that a person has to humble himself before God and repent of their sins for the previous year. On the *final* Feast of Yom Kippur, this will be a permanent and irrevocable decision. This is not a 2nd Chance, but it is the *last chance*. Christians who have studied the 7 Feasts of Israel and the prophetic significance of the last 3 fall Feasts, teach that at this time all persons will be held accountable for his/her sins.

The Battle of Armageddon will be fought on Yom Kippur and the Church Age will end on this day.

And the seventh angel poured out his vial into the air; and there came a great voice out of the temple of heaven, from the throne, saying, It is done   Revelation 16:17

[6] *And I heard as it were the voice of a great multitude, and as the voice of many waters, and as the voice of mighty thunderings, saying, Alleluia: for the Lord God omnipotent reigns*
[7] *Let us be glad and rejoice, and give honor to him: for the marriage of the Lamb is come, and his wife hath made herself ready.*
[8] *And to her was granted that she should be arrayed in fine linen, clean and white: for the fine linen is the righteousness of saints.*
Revelation 19: 6-8

The 1000-Year Millennial Kingdom

Perhaps of equal significance is the belief that on Yom Kippur the long-awaited Messiah of the Jews is expected to establish his earthly kingdom in Jerusalem. Jewish tradition holds that the Feast of Trumpets will begin the 1000-year millennial kingdom of Christ. We believe that they have missed this date by 12 days, and that the Millennial Kingdom will start on Tishri 23 following the *Feast of Tabernacles*. This might be expected since the corporate body of Jews today refuse to accept Christ as their long-awaited Messiah. As the Wrath of God falls upon all unbelievers (including Israel) when the 7-bowl Judgments are poured out, the corporate body of Jews will turn to Jesus Christ and *all of Israel* (who are still alive) *will be saved*. It is crucial that the Jewish belief in their coming Messiah be completely understood. In the Jewish mind, there is much confusion concerning the Messiah which is mentioned many times in the Old Testament.

The Jewish Messiah

In some passages, their Messiah is portrayed as being persecuted and scorned. In other passages He is predicted as a conquering King. To rationalize these conflicting accounts, it is taught that there would *be two messiahs* who were to appear. One is called the *Suffering Servant* or *Messiah Ben Joseph*. The other is seen as a *Conquering King* or *Messiah Ben David*. During His 3.5-year ministry of reconciliation, Jesus Christ taught and healed every day. He was never a ruling King during His earthly ministry, but a suffering servant. The Jews are looking for a Messiah who would serve as both a Suffering Servant and as a conquering King, and they fail to recognize that Jesus Christ our Lord and Savior are both.

This is why almost all orthodox Jews cannot accept Jesus Christ as their long-awaited messiah. In Jewish eyes, Christ was the suffering servant but was never the conquering King. They are eagerly awaiting the appearance of someone (Messiah) who will be both a Suffering Servant and a Conquering King. The arrival of a false Messiah Ben David (Antichrist) will culminate in a great world battle for Jerusalem. The Antichrist will deceive the Jews, and he will be accepted by many as their Messiah when he restores the Jewish Temple as King (dictator) of an European end-time confederacy of nations (Daniel 7). He will enter into a peace treaty with Israel called the *Covenant of Death*. When Satan as the Antichrist invades the temple in Jerusalem, sits upon a throne as Lord and King, and then starts to kill all who will not worship him.... the Jews will they realize that they have been deceived. Only after 3.5 years of *tribulation* will all of Israel realize her error, the *scales will be removed from their eyes*, and they will know that Jesus Christ was both *Messiah Ben Joseph* in His 1st advent, and *Messiah Ben David*. In His 2nd advent. He alone is worthy; He is the only son of the living

God who lived and died as a suffering servant, and He will return again as a conquering King.

All of Israel Will be Saved

And so, all Israel shall be saved: as it is written, there shall come out of Zion the Deliverer, and shall turn away ungodliness from Jacob
Romans 11:26

Jesus lamented of the error of the Jews when he spoke to His disciples on the Mount of Olives just before his crucifixion.

[37] *O Jerusalem, Jerusalem, thou that killed the prophets, and stone them which are sent unto thee, how often would I have gathered thy children together, even as a hen gathers her chickens under her wings, and ye would not!*
[38] *Behold, your house is left unto you desolate.*
[39] *For I say unto you, Ye shall not see me henceforth, till ye shall say, Blessed is he that cometh in the name of the Lord* Matthew 23: 37-39

Hidden from their understanding is how *all Israel* will be *saved* before Christ returns to earth to fight the battle of Armageddon. It is spoken of by Zachariah.

[8] *In that day shall the LORD defend the inhabitants of Jerusalem; and he that is feeble among them at that day shall be as David; and the house of David shall be as God, as the angel of the LORD before them.*
[9] *And it shall come to pass in that day, that I will seek to destroy all the nations that come against Jerusalem.*
[10] *And I will pour upon the house of David, and upon the inhabitants of Jerusalem, the spirit of grace and of supplications: and they shall look upon me whom they have pierced, and they shall mourn for him, as one mourns for his only son, and shall be in bitterness for him, as one that is in bitterness for his firstborn.*
[11] *In that day shall there be a great mourning in Jerusalem, as the*

mourning of Hadadrimmon in the valley of Megiddon
Zechariah 12: 8-11

[1] *In that day there shall be a fountain opened to the house of David and to the inhabitants of Jerusalem for sin and for uncleanness.*
[2] *And it shall come to pass in that day, saith the LORD of hosts, that I will cut off the names of the idols out of the land, and they shall no more be remembered: and I will also cause the prophets and the unclean spirit to pass out of the land.* Zechariah 13: 1-2

[1] *Behold, the day of the LORD cometh, and thy spoil shall be divided in the midst of thee.*
[2] *For I will gather all nations against Jerusalem to battle; and the city shall be taken, and the houses rifled, and the women ravished; and half of the city shall go forth into captivity, and the residue of the people shall not be cut off from the city.*
[3] *Then shall the LORD go forth, and fight against those nations, as when he fought in the day of battle.*
[4] *And his feet shall stand in that day upon the mount of Olives, which is before Jerusalem on the east, and the mount of Olives shall cleave in the midst thereof toward the east and toward the west, and there shall be a very great valley; and half of the mountain shall remove toward the north, and half of it toward the south.*
[5] *And ye shall flee to the valley of the mountains; for the valley of the mountains shall reach unto Azal: yea, ye shall flee, like as ye fled from before the earthquake in the days of Uzziah king of Judah: and the LORD my God shall come, and all the saints with thee.*
[6] *And it shall come to pass in that day, that the light shall not be clear, nor dark:*
[7] **But it shall be one day** *which shall be known to the LORD, not day, nor night: but it shall come to pass, that at evening time it shall be light.*
[8] *And it shall be in that day, that living waters shall go out from Jerusalem; half of them toward the former sea, and half of them toward the hinder sea: in summer and in winter shall it be.*
[9] *And the LORD shall be king over all the earth: in that day shall there*

be one LORD, and his name one.
[10] *All the land shall be turned as a plain from Geba to Rimmon south of Jerusalem: and it shall be lifted up, and inhabited in her place, from Benjamin's gate unto the place of the first gate, unto the corner gate, and from the tower of Hananeel unto the king's winepresses.*
[11] *And men shall dwell in it, and there shall be no more utter destruction; but Jerusalem shall be safely inhabited.*
Zechariah 14: 1-11

The Day of the Lord

There seems to be no doubt about it: **That day** is the **Day of the Lord**, and the great battle being fought is the **Battle of Armageddon** (Phillips, *The Day of the Lord*). The prophet Joel described this day in some detail.

[12] *Let the heathen be wakened, and come up to the valley of Jehoshaphat: for there will I sit to judge all the heathen round about.*
[13] *Put ye in the sickle, for the harvest is ripe: come, get you down; for the press is full, the fats overflow; for their wickedness is great.*
[14] *Multitudes, multitudes in the valley of decision: for the day of the LORD is near in the valley of decision.*
[15] *The sun and the moon shall be darkened, and the stars shall withdraw their shining.*
[16] *The LORD also shall roar out of Zion, and utter his voice from Jerusalem; and the heavens and the earth shall shake: but the LORD will be the hope of his people, and the strength of the children of Israel.*
[17] *So shall ye know that I am the LORD your God dwelling in Zion, my holy mountain: then shall Jerusalem be holy, and there shall no strangers pass through her any more.*
[18] *And it shall come to pass in that day, that the mountains shall drop down new wine, and the hills shall flow with milk, and all the rivers of Judah shall flow with waters, and a fountain shall come forth of the house of the LORD, and shall water the valley of Shittim.*
Joel 3: 12-18

The *Day of the Lord* is when Jesus Christ will descend from heaven and fight the Battle of Armageddon (See Phillips, *The Day of the Lord*). This day is Tishri 10 which is the *Feast of Yom Kippur*. Joel includes several items of great interest to end-time scholars.

- The *Battle of Armageddon* (Revelation 16:15) will take place north and east of *Jerusalem* (Joel 3:17) in the *Valley of Jehosephat* (Joel 3:12)
- This is a harvest of the wicked (Joel 3:13, Revelation 14: 17-20)
- Jesus Christ will fight this battle, but that day is called the *Day of the Lord* (Joel 3:14, Revelation 19: 11-21)
- The sun will not shine and the moon will reflect no light (Joel 3:15, Revelation 6: 12-17, Revelation 16:10)
- On that day, Christ will descend from the heavenly Mt. Zion (Hebrews 12:22), and the earth will shake (Joel 3:16, Revelation 16:18)
- The Lord Jesus Christ will descend to the Mt. of Olives. His feet will split the mountain in half (Zachariah 14:4). Israel will be changed to a great plain (Zachariah 14: 4-10) where Israel will finally inherit the land promised to Abraham, Moses and King David (Ezekiel 36:24,
- The City of Jerusalem will be cleansed, and Jesus Christ will rule and reign for 1000 years from a great Temple which will be built on a great, raised plateau (Isaiah 60:3, Micah 5:2) just north of where Jerusalem stands today …...the new *earthly* Mt. Zion (Joel 3:17, Jeremiah 31: 23-40, Isaiah 60: 10-11
- The land of promise will be fertile and yield its crops (Joel 3:18, Isaiah 11: 6-17, Phillips, *Life After the Great Tribulation*). Even the animal kingdom will change (Isaiah 11: 6-7

- Jesus Christ will rule and reign from His Holy Temple with King David for 1000 years (Jeremiah 30: 3-9, Ezekiel 37:24, Revelation 20:6)

The reader is encouraged to do a short Bible study: Look up every reference to the Day of the Lord in the Bible, and without exception it always refers to a single day. Conversely, practically all of the *pre-tribulation* advocates refer to the *Day of the Lord* as being seven years long. Almost every classical advocate of a *pre-wrath* rapture make the *day of the Lord* 3.5 years long. *What has caused this incorrect interpretation?*

These incorrect interpretations have been caused by four critical mistakes: (1) Incorrectly assuming that the tribulation period was 7 years long (2) not recognizing that the *Wrath of God* is the pouring out of the 7 bowls, immediately following the sounding of the seventh trumpet (Revelation 16:1), and not as the 6th seal is opened (3) failing to recognize that the 7 seals only provide an overview of the tribulation period, (4) failure to distinguish between *wrath* and *tribulation* and (5) refusing to recognize that the rapture of the church occurs at the seventh trump (Phillips, *A New Pre-Wrath Rapture Theory* for a full scriptural justification)

The Feast of Tabernacles (Sukkot)

[34] *Speak unto the children of Israel, saying: The fifteenth day of this seventh month shall be the feast of tabernacles for seven days unto the LORD.*

[36] *Seven days ye shall offer an offering made by fire unto the LORD: on the eighth day shall be a holy convocation unto you; and ye shall offer an offering made by fire unto the LORD: it is a solemn assembly; and ye shall do no servile work therein.*

[39] *Also in the fifteenth day of the seventh month, when ye have gathered in the fruit of the land, ye shall keep a feast unto the LORD seven days: on the first day shall be a sabbath, and on the eighth day shall be a sabbath.*

[40] And ye shall take you on the first day the boughs of goodly trees, branches of palm trees, and the boughs of thick trees, and willows of the brook; and ye shall rejoice before the LORD your God seven days.
[41] And ye shall keep it a feast unto the LORD seven days in the year. It shall be a statute forever in your generations: ye shall celebrate it in the seventh month
[42] Ye shall dwell in booths seven days; all that are Israelites shall dwell in booths   Leviticus 23: 34-42

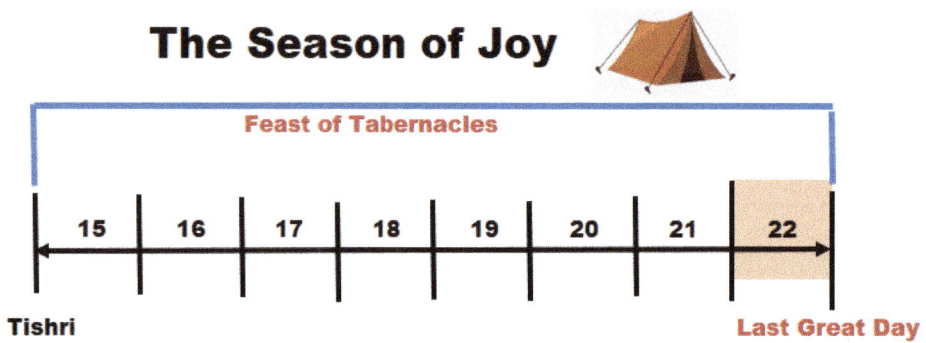

The 8-day *Feast of Tabernacles* is called the *Season of Joy*. The atmosphere of Tabernacles (Feast of Sukkot) was one of rejoicing and celebration. The great Jewish scholar Theodore Gaston has written that no one has experienced such profound and deep joy unless they have attended the Feast of Tabernacles in Jerusalem. The feast is marked by celebration and praise to the Lord for both providing the crop just harvested, and for His provisions of quail, manna, and fresh water throughout the 40-year sojourn of the Exodus in the wilderness. The Feast of Tabernacles is also a celebration that the long growing and harvest season of grain (Barley and Wheat) has come to an end. It corresponds to both the harvest of old grain crops and the subsequent planting of new. It is a time of celebration of the blessings of the Lord. Everything that required hard work was actually a result of God's goodness. Harvest of the Fall crops of wheat, figs and grapes are all completed at this time. The Feast of Tabernacles is one of the three annual Feasts at which every male Hebrew is commanded to attend in Jerusalem. The other two were the *Feast of Passover* and the *Pentecost* (Exodus 23:17, 34:22, Deuteronomy 16:16).

This 7th Holy Feast of Israel commemorates the long nights that each person who fled Egypt in the Exodus slept in tents as they journeyed through the wilderness. After Israel conquered the land of Canaan and began to plant/harvest grain crops it became known as the *Feast of Ingathering*. The Hebrew word for Tabernacles is *temporary dwelling*. The original Tabernacle that Moses built according to the Lord's instructions was a large tent made from gold and other precious metals; the hair of goats; ram's wool died red; and a covering of badger skins. The Lord commanded Israel to observe the 8-day Feast of Tabernacles on Nisan 15-22. The 1st and 8th day of this feast are Holy Days. The Feast of Tabernacles is an 8-day feast, but the *Torah* recognizes Tabernacles as a 7-day feast. The 8th and final day is called *Shmini Atzaret* (Leviticus 23:3 Numbers 29:35) to mark the end of the grain harvests and to thank God for the blessings and abundance of the new grain crops.

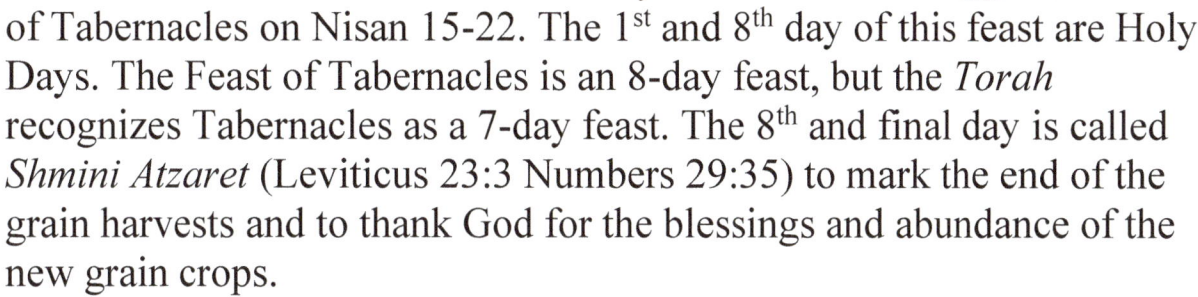

King Solomon dedicated his new temple on the Feast of Tabernacles (I Kings 8:2). The Temple of David was constructed for the Lord to come and *tabernacle* or dwell with man. Tabernacles is the last of the three Fall Feasts. It was one of the three feasts that male Jews were to observe each year (Deuteronomy 16:16) by going to appear before the Lord your God in the place which He shall choose (Jerusalem).

Lighting Candles

The Feast of Tabernacles is initiated at 6:00 PM on Tishri 15 by lighting two candles. Together they represent the overall theme of the Feast. One stands for *Celebrate* and the other *Remember*. Every Jew was commanded to not only remember God's miraculous provisions of food and water in the Wilderness, but also to celebrate inheritance and occupation of the Land of Canaan during the 1000-year Millennial kingdom.

The historical significance of the feast is well understood. It commemorates the Exodus from Egypt, and the 40 years of wandering in the wilderness, in which the Hebrew nation dwelled in temporary tents called *booths*. The feast is sometimes called the *Feast of Booths*. The English equivalent of the Latin word for tabernacle is *hut*. During the seven days between Nisan 15 and Nisan 21, the people live in temporary dwellings typically constructed of palm leaves and willow branches. This is a time of great celebration and introspection of God's goodness. A third name for the full eight-day feast is the *Feast of Ingathering* (Exodus 23:16) to celebrate the abundant harvest of wheat, figs and grapes.

The 8th day

The last day of the feast is called *Shemini Atzeret,* referred to in the scriptures as simply the *eighth day of assembly* (Numbers 29:35). The term Shemini Atzeret is historically interpreted as *tarry or stay another day*. However, the Jewish emphasis on staying one more day as a request is not scripturally correct. The eighth day is ordained by God, and to stay is not an option but a command. The eighth day is primarily directed to the *Tefillat Geshem* or the *prayer for rain* to bless the new crops of grain, figs and olives.

The Water Pouring Ceremony

The Feast of Tabernacles was punctuated by a water-pouring ceremony which occurred every day of the festival. There was a Golden Flask which the High Priest kept upon the altar of sacrifice. Every day the High Priest would walk to the *Pool of Shilom* where the flask would be filled with water. The Pool of Shilom was not just an ordinary body of water, it was fed by an underground spring which was a pure water source that never ran dry. It was water supplied by God, and was appropriate for purification ceremonies. During the Feast of Tabernacles, it was carried to the Temple and poured over the Alter of Sacrifice to consecrate the daily offerings. These rituals were repeated every day between Tishri 15-Tishri 21. Water from the Pool of Siloam symbolized the cleansing and sanctification necessary to prepare one to return to God.

During the seven days beginning on Tishri 15, there were typically three daily acts of praise; (1) the people were to wave branches before the Lord (Leviticus 23); (2) there were daily sacrificial offerings (Numbers 29) and (3) the entire law was to be read in public gatherings. The entire 24 courses of priests were all put into service during this week. Tabernacles is unique in that all nations were invited in ancient times to come up to Jerusalem to worship the Lord alongside the Jewish people. This tradition first arose from the command given to Moses that Israel should sacrifice seventy bulls at Sukkot, which represented the seventy nations descended from Noah (Numbers 29:12-35) which heard the law given by God at Mt. Sinai.

The months following Tishri are particularly critical to a successful planting season and a successful growing season. The *early rains* come during this time and nourish the emerging crops. According to Jewish tradition, God decides at the Feast of Tabernacles on the eighth day whether He will provide abundant rain or little rain in the coming months. The *latter rains* which occurred just before the month of Nisan enables the crops to mature to fullness.

The Lights

The Feast of Tabernacles is sometimes called the *Feast of Lights*. Candles were lighted and placed in all public gathering places and in every window. The candles were to commemorate two miracles of God. The 1st was an ancient Jewish miracle. A small band of Jewish fighters, led by Judah the Maccabee and his family, were in the old Jewish Temple when it was attacked by the Syrian/Greek army. Overmatched in numbers, weapons, and experience it was not expected that they would be able to turn back this huge foe and reclaim the Temple, yet that is exactly what happened. The *Book of Maccabees* recounts how the Jews were led by God to reclaim the desecrated Holy Temple. The second miracle is a miracle of light. The Talmud records that when the victory was secured, the Jews entered the Temple in Jerusalem and found it empty. There was only one small cruse of pure oil, enough to light the menorah in the Temple for one day. But it lasted eight days, remaining lit and never burned out. This miracle is attributed to God and the faith that the Jews had in God. This celebration of light was a shadow and type of our Lord Jesus Christ.

Messianic Application

The first and second coming of our Lord Jesus Christ was equated to the early and latter rains, which clearly reflect the Holy Spirit Falling during his *first advent* and the pouring out of the Spirit of the Lord in the latter days at His *second advent*.

Be patient therefore, brethren, unto the coming of the Lord. Behold, the husbandman waits for the precious fruit of the earth, and hath long patience for it, until he receives the early and latter rain. James 5:7

[28] *And it shall come to pass afterward, that I will pour out my spirit upon all flesh; and your sons and your daughters shall prophesy, your old men shall dream dreams, your young men shall see visions:*
[29] *And also upon the servants and upon the handmaids in those days will I pour out my spirit* Joel 2: 28-29

The Pool of Siloam

The hope that the Lord would be satisfied and produce an abundance of the early and latter rains dominated the temple services each day. Every morning in the temple, the High Priest would go to the *Pool of Siloam* and fill a pitcher full of water. He would return to the temple among the people waving palm branches and reciting Isaiah 12:3: *With joy shall ye draw water out of the wells of salvation.* He would then enter the temple and pour the water out on the *Altar of Sacrifice* as all the people waved palm branches in the air.

It was on the last day of the Feast of Tabernacles (John 7: 2,10) that Jesus Christ rose from the crowd and declared:

[37] In the last day, that great day of the feast, Jesus stood and cried, saying, If any man thirst, let him come unto me, and drink.
[38] He that believeth on me, as the scripture hath said, out of his belly shall flow rivers of living   John 7: 37-38

This was the water that would continuously provide sustenance and never dry up. The Apostle John later wrote that the water of which Jesus spoke was typed by the *Holy Spirit* which now dwells in every Born-Again believer (John 7:39).

The first day of the feast (Tishri 15) and the last day of the feast (Tishri 22) are both *High Sabbaths*. There could be no work done on these days, and Jewish civil laws restricted travel to a Sabbath-day's journey, which was defined as 2000 cubits (about 22 miles). The cool evenings during this time were a time of pure joy. Tradition has it that no celebration in all of ancient Israel could compare to that which took place during the Feast of Tabernacles, and no single day could compare to the last day. The rabbis wrote: *He that hath not beheld the joy of this celebration had never experienced real joy in his life* (Joseph Good).

Jesus was undoubtedly referring to this joy when He spoke of the light that He can bring to all people who believe upon His name.

Then spoke Jesus again unto them, saying, I am the light of the world: he that follows me shall not walk in darkness, but shall have the light of life   John 8:12

The Coronation of Jesus Christ

Immediately preceding the 1000-Year Millennial Kingdom, the Feast of Tabernacles will celebrate the coronation of Jesus Christ to rule and reign with King David during the Millennial Kingdom. There will be great rejoicing and praise because: *the kingdoms of this world will have become the kingdoms of our Lord Jesus Christ*. (Revelation 11:15). All believers will be required to attend the Feast of Tabernacles every year

(Zachariah 14:16). The Hebrews will inherit the land promised to them long ago; the saints will rule and reign with Christ; and the earth will yield its fruit and crops in abundance, Every Jewish inhabitant will sit under his own fig tree (I Kings 4:25).

A detailed study of the Feast of Tabernacles is both an enlightening and rewarding study. There are many shadows and types of Jesus Christ in this eight-day feast. The Feast of Tabernacles has significant application to the second coming of Jesus Christ and His initiation of the millennial kingdom. After His 2nd advent and the Battle of Armageddon; the 144,000 Hebrews who have been sealed to enter the millennial kingdom; the remnant who have survived the 7 Bowl Judgments; survivors of the Sheep and Goat judgment; the Bride of Christ and all glorified believers will rest in future Feasts of Tabernacles. It is also interesting that of all the Seven Feasts, *only* the Feast of Tabernacles is mentioned as being held during the 1000-year Millennial Kingdom.

Future Feast of Tabernacles

In the future (during the 1000-year Millennial Kingdom, *all* families of the earth will be *required* to come to Jerusalem to annually celebrate the Feast of Tabernacles). The penalty for not attending will be that God will withhold the rain from their crops. (Zechariah 14: 16-19). God is setting up His kingdom......He will rule as a righteous monarch and he is going to rule and reign with Both King David and the saints. Jews living in a Land of Promise, setting under their own fig tree in their own land, and fully occupying the land of Canaan is a promise to Israel which must be fulfilled.

[16] And it shall come to pass, that every one that is left of all the nations which came against Jerusalem shall even go up from year to year to worship the King, the LORD of hosts, and to keep the Feast of Tabernacles.
[17] And it shall be, that whoso will not come up of all the families of the earth unto Jerusalem to worship the King, the LORD of hosts, even upon them shall be no rain.

[18] *And if the family of Egypt go not up, and come not, that have no rain; there shall be the plague, wherewith the LORD will smite the heathen that come not up to keep the Feast of Tabernacles.*
[19] *This shall be the punishment of Egypt, and the punishment of all nations that come not up to keep the feast of tabernacles.*
Zechariah 14: 16-19

God will require that all nations attend the Feast of Tabernacles every year. Failure to do so will result in *no rain* and *a plague* to Fall upon all those who do not obey His command.

Part IV
The Future Revealed

We have given an overview of the four Spring Feasts and the three Fall Feasts of Israel. All seven Feasts are *rehearsals* for seven *appointments* that have been ordained since time began for our Lord Jesus Christ. The first four (Spring) Feasts were fulfilled at the 1st advent of Christ, and the last three (Fall) Feasts will be fulfilled at the Rapture and the 2nd advent of Christ. Collectively, all seven Feasts provide a *blueprint* for the work that Christ will accomplish. They also provide a blueprint of how the tribulation period will end. In particular, it is our uncompromising belief that at the last Feast of Trumpets, Christ will appear in the air and the *rapture* will occur: The *Battle of Armageddon* will occur on the Feast of Yom Kippur: The Feast of tabernacles will celebrate the victory over Satan at Armageddon: and the *1000-year Millennial Kingdom*. The last three Feasts of Israel predict the future.

The Rapture
The rapture of all the saints (living and dead) was described by Paul. It will take place as the last trumpet is blown (Rams horn)

[51] *Behold, I shew you a mystery; We shall not all sleep, but we shall all be changed,*
[52] *In a moment, in the twinkling of an eye, at the last trump: for the trumpet shall sound, and the dead shall be raised incorruptible, and we shall be changed.*
[53] *For this corruptible must put on incorruption, and this mortal must put on immortality.*
[54] *So when this corruptible shall have put on incorruption, and this mortal shall have put on immortality, then shall be brought to pass the saying that is written, Death is swallowed up in victory.*   I Corinthians 15: 51-54

The Battle of Armageddon

At the last Feast of Yom Kippur, Christ will return again, this time upon the earth and not in the sky. He will descend to the Mount of Olives to fight the battle of Armageddon.

[1] *Behold, the day of the LORD cometh, and thy spoil shall be divided in the midst of thee.*
[2] *For I will gather all nations against Jerusalem to battle; and the city shall be taken, and the houses rifled, and the women ravished; and half of the city shall go forth into captivity, and the residue of the people shall not be cut off from the city.*
[3] *Then shall the LORD go forth, and fight against those nations, as when he fought in the day of battle.*
[4] *And his feet shall stand in that day upon the mount of Olives, which is before Jerusalem on the east, and the mount of Olives shall cleave in the midst thereof toward the east and toward the west, and there shall be a very great valley; and half of the mountain shall remove toward the north, and half of it toward the south.*
[5] *And ye shall flee to the valley of the mountains; for the valley of the mountains shall reach unto Azal: yea, ye shall flee, like as ye fled from before the earthquake in the days of Uzziah king of Judah: and the LORD my God shall come, and all the saints with thee.*
[6] *And it shall come to pass in that day, that the light shall not be clear, nor dark:*
[7] *But it shall be one day which shall be known to the LORD, not day, nor night: but it shall come to pass, that at evening time it shall be light.*
[8] *And it shall be **in that day**, that living waters shall go out from Jerusalem; half of them toward the former sea, and half of them toward the hinder sea: in summer and in winter shall it be.*
[9] *And the LORD shall be king over all the earth: in that day shall there be one LORD, and his name one.*
[10] *All the land shall be turned as a plain from Geba to Rimmon south of Jerusalem: and it shall be lifted up, and inhabited in her place, from Benjamin's gate unto the place of the first gate, unto the corner gate, and from the tower of Hananeel unto the king's winepresses.*

[11] *And men shall dwell in it, and there shall be no more utter destruction; but Jerusalem shall be safely inhabited.*
[12] *And this shall be the plague wherewith the LORD will smite all the people that have fought against Jerusalem; Their flesh shall consume away while they stand upon their feet, and their eyes shall consume away in their holes, and their tongue shall consume away in their mouth.*
Zechariah 14: 1-12

[11] *And I saw heaven opened, and behold a white horse; and he that sat upon him was called Faithful and True, and in righteousness he doth judge and make war.*
[12] *His eyes were as a flame of fire, and on his head were many crowns; and he had a name written, that no man knew, but he himself.*
[13] *And he was clothed with a vesture dipped in blood: and his name is called The Word of God.*
[14] *And the armies which were in heaven followed him upon white horses, clothed in fine linen, white and clean.*
[15] *And out of his mouth goeth a sharp sword, that with it he should smite the nations: and he shall rule them with a rod of iron: and he treads the winepress of the fierceness and wrath of Almighty God.*
[16] *And he hath on his vesture and on his thigh a name written, KING OF KINGS, AND LORD OF LORDS.* Revelation 19: 11-16

The Last Feast
The Feast of Tabernacles is the 7th and last Feast of Israel. It starts 5 days after the Feast of Yom Kippur which ends the Church Age and is when Christ will return to fight the Battle of Armageddon. It is a joyous feast of celebration that will probably start the 1000-year millennial Kingdom. It is a festival where the Menorah is lit every day to celebrate the rededication of the Temple following Judas Maccabeus's victory over the Seleucids. According to rabbinic tradition, the victorious Maccabees could only find a small jug of oil that had remained pure and uncontaminated, and although it only contained enough oil to sustain the Menorah for one day, it miraculously lasted for eight days. A water pouring ceremony is held every day for the first 7 days to celebrate how

God provided water in the wilderness for 40 years during the Exodus from Egypt. All male Jews are required to attend this festival, and for 7 nights they sleep in a tabernacle (tent) just as Israel did during the Exodus. The 8th and final day of the Feast of Tabernacles is possibly the greatest celebration and festival during each year. The 8th day celebrates the redemption of Israel from sin and transgression by their long-awaited messiah. It is also a celebration looking forwards to a day when Israel will inherit the land of promise and live in peace. The realization of this expectation is the 1000-year Millennial Kingdom. The 1000-year millennial kingdom will be populated by the *earthly seed of Abraham*, and the saints who are the *starry seed of Abraham* will rule and reign with Christ for 1000 years.

I am often asked the following question: *when will the rapture of the church occur?* To the amazement of everyone listening; *On some future Feast of Trumpets, in the month of September or October*. To you the reader we urge you to *watch and wait, for the time is surely near*. It is hopeless and foolish to predict a date when our Lord Jesus Christ will return for His body (Matthew 24:36), which is the church of all born again believers: But it is not foolish to determine the time or the season.

The Spring Feasts (fulfilled @ Jesus' first coming)				Feast Gap Period (fulfilled by Church Age)	The Autumn (Fall) Feasts (fulfilled @ Jesus' second coming)		
Passover	Unleavened Bread	FirstFruits	Pentecost		Trumpets	Atonement	Tabernacles
Crucifixion Of Jesus	Burial Of Jesus	Resurrection Of Jesus	Coming of the Holy Spirit		Rapture & Resurrection Of Believers	Second Coming Of Jesus	Messianic Kingdom Age
Nisan 14	Nisan 15-22	Nisan 17	Sivan 7		Tishri 1	Tishri 10	Tishri 15-22
Exodus 12 Matt 26:17-27	Lev 23:6-8 I Cor 5:7-8	Lev 23:9-14 I Cor 15:20-23	Lev 23:15-22 Acts 1 & 2		Lev 23:23-25 1 Cor 15:51-52	Lev 23:26-32 Matt 24:29-30	Lev 23:33-44 Rev 20:1-6

——— 'The Days of Awe' ———
Time of Jacob's trouble

The Seven Feasts of Israel

The Spring Feasts

Feast	Date	Prophetic Significance
Passover	Nisan 14	Redemption and Salvation. Christ was our perfect Passover lamb. The New Covenant replaces the Old Covenant
Unleavened Bread	Nisan 15-Nisan 21	Justification and Sanctification. Christ was without sin. He is the bread of life
FirstFruits	First Sunday of Unleavened Bread	Resurrection and life. Christ rose from the grave and conquered death
Weeks	Starts on Feast of Firstfruits and Lasts 49 days. 50th day is Pentecost	Sanctification and spiritual maturity. The Holy Spirit fell on the Day of Pentecost

The Fall Feasts

Feast	Date	Prophetic Significance
Trumpets	Tishri 1	Rapture of the Saints and Resurrection of the Dead. Wedding of the Lamb. Bema Seat Judgement
Yom Kippur	Tishri 10	Second Coming of Christ. Judgment of the Nations. Satan cast into Bottomless Pit for 1000 years. Antichrist and False Prophet cast into Lake of Fire
Tabernacles	Tishri 15- Tishri 21. Tishri 22 is a High Sabbath and a fast day	Beginning of 1000 year Millennial Kingdom. Tribulation Martyrs Raised. Judgement of the Nations

This concludes our study of the 7 Feasts of Israel.

Bibliography

Coulter, Fred R., The Appointed Times of Jesus the Messiah, York Publishing Company, PO Box 1038, Hollister, California, 95024-1038

Coulter, Fred R., The Death of Jesus the Christ, York Publishing Company, PO Box 1038, Hollister, California, 95024-1038

Dake, Finis J., Dake's Annotated Reference Bible, Dake Bible Sales, P.O. Box 1050, Lawrenceville, Ga., 30246

Finegan, Jack, Handbook of Biblical Chronology, Hendrickson Publishing Company, Peabody, Ma.

Good, Joseph, Rosh Hashanah and the Messianic Kingdom to Come, Hatikva Ministries, PO Box 3125, Port Arthur, Texas 77643-0703

Horn H. S. and L. H. Wood, The Chronology of Ezra, TEACH Services, Inc., www.teachservices.com

Larkin, Clarence, Dispensational Truth, P.O. Box 334, Glenside, Pa., 1920

Logos apostolic Church of God and Bible College, Interlinear Greek and Hebrew Translation, Logos apostolic.org, United Kingdom, Logos apostolic.org

Nee, Watchman, Come Lord Jesus, Christian Fellowship Publishers, Inc., 11515 Allecingie Parkway, Richmond, Virginia 23235

Phillips, Don T., The Book of Revelation: *Mysteries Revealed*, 2nd Edition, Virtual Bookworm. com, PO Box 9949, College Station, Tx, 77845

Phillips, Don T., The Book of Ruth: *Historical and Prophetic Truths*, Virtual Bookworm. com, PO Box 9949, College Station, Tx, 77845

Phillips, Don T., Life After Death: *Mysteries Revealed*, Virtual Bookworm. com, PO Box 9949, College Station, Tx, 77845

Phillips, Don T., The Eternal Plan of God: *Dispensations, Covenant Promises, Salvation*, Virtual Bookworm. com, PO Box 9949, College Station, Texas 7784.

Phillips, Don T., *The Birth and Death of Christ*, Virtual Bookworm. com, PO Box 9949, College Station, Tx, 77845

Phillips, Don T., The Book of Exodus: *Historical and Prophetic Truths* Virtual Bookworm. com, PO Box 9949, College Station, Tx, 77845

Phillips, Don T., A Biblical Chronology from Adam to Christ, Virtual Bookworm. com, PO Box 9949, College Station, Tx, 77845

Phillips, Don T., Life After the Great Tribulation: *The Millennial Kingdom,* Virtual Bookworm. com, PO Box 9949, College Station, Tx, 77845

Phillips, Don T., The Last 50 Days of Jesus Christ Virtual Bookworm. com, PO Box 9949, College Station, Tx, 77845

Phillips, Don T., The Daniel 70 Week Prophecy Virtual Bookworm. com, PO Box 9949, College Station, Texas 77845

Phillips, Don T., The Day of the Lord Virtual Bookworm. com, PO Box 9949, College Station, Texas 77845

Phillips, Don T., The Birth of Christ: *A Forensic Analysis*
Virtual Bookworm. com, PO Box 9949, College Station, Tx, 77845

Phillips, Don T., The Wrath and Judgments of God
Virtual Bookworm. com, PO Box 9949, College Station, Texas 77845

Phillips, Don T., Biblical Truths about Difficult Concepts
Virtual Bookworm. com, PO Box 9949, College Station, Texas 77845

Phillips, Don T., A New Pre-Wrath Rapture Theory
Virtual Bookworm. com, PO Box 9949, College Station, Texas 77845

Phillips, Don T., Rapture and Resurrection: *The Blessed Hope of All Believers,* Virtual Bookworm. com, PO Box 9949, College Station, Texas 77845

Rosenthal, Matthew, The Pre-Wrath Rapture of the Church, Thomas Nelson Publishers, Nashville, Tennessee

Ryrie, Charles C., The Ryrie Study Bible, King James Version, Moody Press, Chicago. Ill

Salerno, Donald A., Revelation Unsealed, Virtual Bookworm.Com, P.O. Box 9949, College Station, Texas, 77842

Thiele, Edwin R., The Mysterious Numbers of the Hebrew Kings: *Revised Edition*, Kregel, Grand Rapids, Michigan

Thomas, Robert L., Revelation 1-7, An Exegetical Commentary, Moody Press, Chicago, Illinois

Thomas, Robert L., Revelation 8-22, An Exegetical Commentary, Moody Press, Chicago, Illinois

Van Kampen, Robert, The Sign, Crossway Books, 1300 Crescent Street, Wheaton, Illinois 60187

Walvoord, John F., The Millennial Kingdom, Academic Books, Zondervan Publishing Company, 1415 Lake Drive S.E., Grand Rapids, Michigan 49506

Footnote:

This manuscript has drawn upon several excellent websites found by GOOGLE search. It is my intention to recognize every biblical scholar and source of information from those *giants that walked before me*. This information was sometimes not made available. In other cases, information was marked open source or not marked at all. If any author(s) sees any material that they want referenced, please contact me and I will acknowledge their previous research and scholarly work. In any case, I am extremely grateful for previous investigations or conclusions that may (or may not) support this work. God will know them and He will know the source.

> Don T. Phillips
> Senior Author
> phillipsdon60@gmail.com

> Spring, 2023

www.ingramcontent.com/pod-product-compliance
Lightning Source LLC
Chambersburg PA
CBHW060950170426
43202CB00026B/3001